FLYING
REBEL

The Royal Air Force Museum, Hendon

FLYING REBEL

THE STORY OF

LOUIS STRANGE

Peter Hearn

Foreword by Sir Peter Masefield

London: HMSO

© Peter Hearn 1994
Applications for reproduction should be made to HMSO

ISBN 0 11 290500 5

Jacket illustrations: *front* – excerpt from the 1959 *Top Spot* cartoon of the famous Martinsyde incident (pp 46–8); *inside flap* – Louis Strange in the rank of Squadron Leader whilst commanding the Parachute Training School (painting by Eric Kennington, courtesy of The RAF Museum, Hendon).

Frontispiece: Strange prepares to fly his own company's Spartan Arrow in one of the many air races in which he took part – and sometimes won – during the golden age of flying in the 1930s.

Author and publisher have attempted, so far without success, to trace the artist whose realistic drawings for *Top Spot* show Louis Strange in action, on the front of the jacket and in the book. They wish to thank the artist for his work; and Whitakers, the Publisher's Association, the Association of Illustrators and the Design, Artists and Copyright Society for their assistance in the search. If the legal copyright holders in question wish to contact HMSO, we shall ensure that the correct acknowledgement appears in any future edition of this book.

HMSO publications are available from:

HMSO Publications Centre
(Mail, fax and telephone orders only)
PO Box 276, London, SW8 5DT
Telephone orders 071-873 9090
General enquiries 071-873 0011
(queuing system in operation for both numbers)
Fax orders 071-873 8200

HMSO Bookshops
49 High Holborn, London, WC1V 6HB
(counter service only)
071-873 0011 Fax 071-873 8200
258 Broad Street, Birmingham, B1 2HE
021-643 3740 Fax 021-643 6510
33 Wine Street, Bristol, BS1 2BQ
0272-264306 Fax 0272-294515
9–21 Princess Street, Manchester, M60 8AS
061-834 7201 Fax 061-833 0634
16 Arthur Street, Belfast, BT1 4GD
0232-238451 Fax 0232-235401
71 Lothian Road, Edinburgh, EH3 9AZ
031-228 4181 Fax 031-229 2734

HMSO'S Accredited Agents
(see Yellow Pages)

and through good booksellers

CONTENTS

FOREWORD
by Sir Peter Masefield

Here is a book to be savoured and enjoyed. Its subject, Louis Strange, was one of that elite band of pioneer airmen who combined exceptional flying skills with unquenchable enthusiasm and – in the words of Stephen Spender – 'left the vivid air signed with their honour'.

Group Captain Peter Hearn delightfully brings to life the essence of the spirited approach, the devotion to good airmanship, and the irrepressible 'get up and go' eccentricity of Louis Strange. For almost half a century – from the time he learned to fly at Hendon in 1913 until the age of sixty-eight (when he flew himself from Thruxton to RAF Coltishall, typically for a squadron reunion) – Strange revelled in action, flew with gusto, cheerfully rebelled against the rigid order of things, and endeared himself to a host of friends and colleagues, though not always to higher authority.

Of all the remarkable and forthright characters who embellished the formative years of aviation, none was more dedicated and enterprising than the young Louis Arbon Strange. Having already established himself as one of the famous 'Hendon fliers' he joined the Royal Flying Corps in 1914 to become an immensely courageous and inventive pioneer of aerial combat.

I first met him in 1932, by which time, having retired from the RAF ten years earlier, he had become a prominent figure in civil aviation. In that golden age of light-aeroplane manufacture and sporting flying 'Colonel Strange', as he was generally known, was a familiar and popular presence at aerodromes throughout the British Isles and Europe. He was director, demonstration pilot and salesman for the newly formed Simmonds Aircraft Ltd and at our first meeting he extolled to me the virtues of his company's tri-motor Spartan Cruiser. A year later when Whitney Straight and I flew to that historic centre of motor sport and aviation at Brooklands, there to greet us was Louis Strange, demonstrating a new Spartan Arrow to Duncan Davies of the Brooklands Flying School. When he subsequently joined Whitney to control and operate Straight Corporation's regional airports, Louis entered his new enterprise with customary zeal and was to be seen everywhere, flying and promoting the 'airfaring outlook' to a widening circle of friends.

It was typical of Louis Strange that although he was officially too old at forty-nine for flying duties in the Second World War, he found his way back into the cockpit by a determined pulling of strings and embarked upon a series of extraordinary adventures which would have seemed far-fetched even in the pages of pre-war *Boys' Own* annuals, including the celebrated Hurricane escape from France – told here so effectively in his own words – and the pioneering of parachute training. In this outstanding biography, Peter Hearn's own close association with airborne forces lends special authority to his assessment of Louis Strange's crucial role in the genesis of British parachute troops.

Those who served with Louis Strange testify in this book to the exceptional and endearing qualities of the man. 'It was quite an experience serving under Louis. He was, above all, human and kind – but quite dotty,' recalls one. To his great friend and colleague of both world wars, the famous Robert Smith Barry, Louis Strange was quite simply 'the bravest man in the world'.

For a further seven years after the war, Strange returned to the aviation scene to contribute to the revival of British light-aeroplane flying, as a much respected figure. But, from the early 1950s, bereft of the stimulus of action which had meant so much to his life, he was sadly overtaken by advancing physical and mental disabilities.

Peter Hearn treats with delicacy and understanding this final epoch in the life of an exceptional man. The story of Louis Strange's extraordinary career would have been lost to later generations but for this meticulous, vivid and highly readable biography, which recaptures so well the spirited and gusty nature of a *Flying Rebel*.

I heartily commend this important contribution to aeronautical history, which general and specialist readers alike will find enthralling. Read and enjoy it.

PREFACE

Louis Strange? Oh yes, aviation buffs will say, wasn't he the chap who had that amazing tussle with an inverted Martinsyde in the First World War? And who won a bar to his DFC in the Second by that incredible escapade in a Hurricane? Yes, that was the man.

It would amuse Louis Strange to be remembered for those oft-quoted adventures. For him, they were the stuff of flying – far more important than the dry facts of aviation history. Nor were they isolated incidents, for his was a life packed with aerial adventure and achievement. A life that encompassed more than fifty years of active flying in 115 aircraft types, from the Grahame-White Box-Kite of 1913 to the Venom jet-fighter of 1955. A life devoted to the encouragement of what he termed the 'spirit of air adventure'. A life marked by an endearing disregard for authority. A life that deserves a more prominent place in the story of flight. A life that it is my privilege and pleasure to record.

In writing the story of Louis Strange, I am indebted to the man himself. He abhorred bumf, and retained hardly any. What he did leave, however, were the rather tattered manuscripts, not only of his published book, *Recollections of an Airman*, but also of three unpublished works relating his family history and his own early life, his years farming and flying during the 1920s and 1930s, and his experiences during the Second World War. Because his own words tell of the man as well as his deeds, I have used them extensively throughout this biography. I have also drawn on his surviving log-books. They were not well kept: they contain many omissions, some factual errors, results of some of his steeplechasing, and occasional notes to himself. Two were lost. He obviously classed them as bumf. It was the flying that was important to Louis Strange, not the recording of it.

To his own source material was added an immaculate and comprehensive scrap-book of memorabilia: photographs, newspaper cuttings, magazine articles, programmes, commendations, letters, obituaries. The collection presents the story of Louis Strange in word and picture, from earliest days until his death in 1966. This was not the work of Louis, nor of his family, but of his friend, the late H 'Fitz' Cowley. It is a tribute not only to Louis Strange, but to one man's admiration for another. This biography would have been a poor thing without it, and the scrap-book now forms the centre-piece of the Louis Strange Collection in the Royal Air Force Museum, Hendon.

I never met Louis Strange, and am therefore indebted to those who knew him for portraying the man so vividly, and for providing more anecdotes than I could put into a single volume. Above all I am grateful to Sir Peter Masefield, who from his knowledge of Louis Strange as a fellow pilot of the 1930s and as a prominent figure in aviation since that time, has provided a generous foreword to this biography. Others who have contributed from their personal knowledge of Louis Strange are Harry Ward, Robert Fender, Cyril Tubbs, Air Vice-Marshal Tony Dudgeon, Richard Townshend Bickers, Air Marshal Michael Lyne, Peter Mallet, Alec Lumsden, John Pickwell, John McDonald and G C Pinkerton.

All illustrations are from the Louis Strange Archive, held at the Royal Air Force Museum, unless otherwise acknowledged.

I have supplemented original material with comment, information and anecdote from the annals of aviation history, as gratefully acknowledged in the references. Those outstanding aviation historians Jack Bruce and Chaz Bowyer have pointed me in right directions, and Jack was kind enough to comment most constructively on those chapters relating Louis Strange's First World War.

I am also grateful for assistance and information provided by Graham Austin of the Merchant Ships Fighter Unit (MSFU) Association, Major John R Cross of the Museum of Army Flying, Peter Elliot and his staff at the RAF Museum, Michael Goodall, Mike Hatch of the Air Historical Branch, Thomas R Hiett, Reg Leach of the Manchester Airport Archives, David Shepherd, Gordon Simons of GMS Enterprises and Squadron Leader George Sizeland of No. 1 Parachute Training School (PTS).

Dr Michael Fopp, as Director of the Royal Air Force Museum, gave early encouragement to this biography and was instrumental in achieving its publication by sponsoring and recommending the project to HMSO. The co-operation and editorial advice I have received from Ruth Bowden of HMSO and from Bridget Lely has been heartening and most valuable.

Finally, I am grateful to members of the Strange family for the assistance, understanding and hospitality extended to me during the writing of this story: Louis's neice Mrs Vecta Mitchell, his great-nephews David, Ronald and John Strange, and in particular his daughter Susan Strange. Without her encouragement and material support, the story of Louis Arbon Strange would not have been written.

CHAPTER ONE

All Because of a Sheep with Footrot . . .

There were two freshly dug graves in the churchyard at Magny, 3 miles north-east of Bayeux. On the wooden cross above one hung the helmet of a British soldier. On the other cross was a German helmet. There were flowers on both graves.

The British soldier – explained the verger to the lean, hawk-faced officer beside him – had been shot as he had come down the lane, by a sniper hidden in the belfry. The sniper had been hit by return fire, and had fallen to his death on the altar steps. The villagers had buried the two side by side.

The British officer, looking down on the graves, prayed for the sake of young men like these that this war would not be long in drawing to its close. It was the second world war in which he had fought, and although he had served in both with verve and distinction, he wanted it over. He turned, and crossed the churchyard to the battered rectory where he had set up his headquarters: Advanced HQ No. 46 Group, Royal Air Force, tasked with providing support for the Allied invasion of Normandy. It was June 1944. The man was Wing Commander Louis Arbon Strange.

The following Sunday, Louis Strange found time to attend the morning service at the church. Amongst the congregation he recognised the farmer on whose land the British had hacked out and bulldozed the landing-strip for the Dakotas of 46 Group. The farmer had helped them. When the planes had started flying in with supplies, and out again with casualties, he and his wife had appeared with churns of fresh milk for the wounded troops. The man now smiled at the Wing Commander.

'Commandant Strange?'

'Yes.'

'I also am a Strange,' said the Norman farmer. 'My name is Étrange, Monsieur Étrange.'

The two men shook hands. Later, in the evening, and for several evenings after that, Louis Strange went through the high stone archway and across the great yard to the long, low farmhouse that flanked the far side of it. There, with the rumble of war coming to

1

them from the direction of Caen, sometimes from much closer, sometimes from the air above, Louis Strange reached back into his own ancestry, as related by Monsieur Étrange, the farmer of Normandy . . .

In 1065, Jean Étrange, blacksmith on this very land, was being pestered by his son. The boy wanted to join the force being gathered to cross the seas for the invasion of England. No, Jean Étrange had said: the lad could not be spared from the forge. But the skill of the blacksmith and his son as makers of arrow-heads as well as ploughshares was known. The youth was also a good bow-man. Jean Étrange was persuaded – by Duke William himself it was said – to release the lad to the army. So across the sea in 1066, as archer and arrow-maker to William, went the son of Jean Étrange, to fight the British on a hillside called Hastings. It was the custom for bow-men to burn their names on selected arrow-shafts so that a reward might be claimed should they find a target of high degree. It was still held in those parts of Normandy that the name on the shaft that pierced the eye of Harold, the English King, was that of Étrange.

After the Conquest, young Étrange had remained in England, to farm land granted to him by William in what was to become Sussex. His name had been Louis. Louis Étrange.

Now, almost 900 years later, another Louis Strange, also a warrior, also a farmer, had crossed the sea in the opposite direction with another invading army. And had uncovered his roots.

Louis Arbon Strange had always assumed Norman ancestry. With a name like that, and with uncles called Robert and Roger, how could it be otherwise? As a boy he had been deeply ashamed of his names and of the French connection of which they spoke. A great fear of Napoleon and of the French had been instilled in his earliest recollections by the stories of how his great-grandfather had taken the Yeomanry to Weymouth to stem the expected invasion by the dreaded 'Boney', whose guardsmen were said to be seven feet tall.

He had not been able to trace the family as far back as young Louis Étrange, archer and arrow-maker to William the Conqueror, but could track it with certainty to the early seventeenth century, when the Stranges were well established on Sussex land. By the eighteenth century, Joseph Strange had developed fine orchards and became known as 'Appledram Joe' from the quality of his cider. His three sons, Samuel, John and Robert, became champions of all England at singlesticks in 1735 when they beat three brothers from Yorkshire in bloody and bruising battle. Samuel was a wild one. His

2

wife would put him in the stocks each Saturday night to sober him for church on Sunday. 'Little' John – six feet three – farmed in Dorsetshire, in the valley of the Stour. He was renowned as a fine judge of sheep and cattle, which he bought and sold by the hundred throughout the south and south-west. He once walked a bull, with iron tips on its hooves, the 80 miles from Spetisbury to Oxford, to win at the Royal Show.

The battling instincts of the Stranges had surfaced again in Roger Strange, who farmed at South Mundham in the late nineteenth century. He was a noted fighter of the bare-knuckle days. In a bout staged for the benefit of a house-party by Mr Radcliffe at the Hyde, he had fought the great Jem Mace. The former British champion was past his prime, but he laid Roger's cheek open to the bone before the younger man had beaten him into a bloody mess. Twenty-five pounds had gone into the hat to be shared between them.

It was to the farm at Spetisbury, where 'Little' John had raised his stock over a hundred years before, that Louis Arbon Strange was born in 1891.

From his father Walter John Strange, known as John, the young Louis heard of the great bonfire on top of Bulbarrow, where the workers had burnt the new labour-saving reapers; of the great frost of 1840, when the Stour had frozen and no coaches ran between Weymouth and London for three months, and of the consternation that greeted the opening of the railway between Poole and Bath – for surely, said the country folk, the sparks would set fire to the corn ricks and thatched roofs for miles around, in spite of the cage over the monster's funnel . . .

John Strange was a caring farmer, with a true love of the land and a simple philosophy of putting back into the soil more than was taken out of it. He was primarily a dairy farmer. The land must improve the animals, and the animals must improve the land, he would tell Louis. The boy's mother was also of a long-established farming heritage. Her grandfather, a famed horseman, had grazed his hunters on fields at Hendon on the northern outskirts of London. From those very fields, many years later, his grandson would take to the air in the earliest flying machines.

This landed and vigorous ancestry generated a love of the soil, an adventurous nature and a fierce independence of spirit that were to guide Louis Arbon Strange throughout his life, on the land and in the air.

Home for the young Louis was the mill-house of Tarrant Keyneston Mill, on the River Stour. It was a working mill, administered by his father, and run by Charles Wellen and his son

George. The regular and reassuring beat of the giant wheel rocked the boy to sleep at nights, and its strange silence laid more emphasis on his Sundays than did the three visits to church. Church was 200 yards down the lane, opposite the rectory, which 'was of more importance to the children of the village than Buckingham Palace. The Reverend Samuel Walker was the Lord God Jehovah and all the prophets rolled into one, while Mrs Walker was a kind of Queen Mother.' [1]

It was a contented and peaceful community in which the boy was raised. A close-knit community, closely linked with the land and its seasons. For a young boy there was the hill behind Tarrant Abbey for tobogganing in winter; the marvel of calving, and sprouting crops in spring; hay-making in summer; the steam-thresher and its crew moving from farm to farm in autumn; and at all seasons the working of the mill to wonder at. And there were country characters to grow up with, like:

> Steve Marchment's father who, as far as I knew never did anything but catch rabbits on Abbeycroft Down. He was a very tall fine man with a big beard. He always wore a long coat with huge pockets and carried nets and ferrets, and rabbits which he produced like a magician. We thought of him as one, for he always held his finger to his lips to stop our chatter and never spoke a word himself. I expect that was because silence and quiet were essential to his calling. [1]

Above all, there was riding. When Louis was six, his father bought a pony. Louis and his elder brother Ronald were sat bareback upon it. On a long rein, their father set the pony trotting round a freshly ploughed piece of ground. Inevitably they fell off, onto the softened earth. It was this chastening experience, Louis was to say, that probably made Ronald decide to become a sailor. Louis climbed back on. Riding was to become one of the loves of his life.

In addition to Ronald, there was an older sister, Daisy, who married when Louis was eleven and who was suitably remote from him. By then, Ronald was at sea, beginning a career that would take him to a Master's ticket at the age of twenty-four and distinction in the Royal Navy. Louis had little time for his younger sisters Stephanie and Ruth, but doted over his young brother Ben, who was destined to die in the air over Cambrai in 1918.

School for the young Louis Strange was Cliff House prep school, and St Edward's, Oxford – where another great airman, Douglas Bader, would later receive his schooling. It was a more expensive education than the son of a working farmer could expect: better than that provided for the children of wealthier local families. Louis was ever grateful to his parents for his schooling. He was an adequate

M. Pead. Oakfield Studio, Blandford.

Louis Arbon Strange in 1902, aged eleven

scholar, and a promising sportsman. At St Edward's he created a new record for the under-sixteen mile; rowed for his House; played cricket for the School Eleven, and rugby for the Second Fifteen. At sixteen he returned to Dorset and to farming.

A believer in early responsibility, John Strange put the youngster in charge of 600 acres and a dairy herd at Lower Almer Farm. Louis had inherited his father's caring attitude towards land and stock, but although guided by his parent and by the earthy wisdom of the hands assigned to him, he was soon demonstrating a powerful streak of initiative and independence. He read everything about dairy farming that he could lay hands on, and was amongst the first in the county to number his cows and heifers with a hot-iron on their horns so that he could weigh and record their milk yields.

His life was that of most young farmers of Edwardian England's southern counties: hard work whenever called for, but plenty of fun and recreation as well. There was the normal country round of weddings and christenings, fairs and markets; dances in the winter, picnics in the summer; a shoot at least once a week and always a party to follow; cricket for the village team; fishing competitions and clay-pigeon shooting; tennis, which had recently replaced croquet as the foremost social sport, and visits to London to stay with his Aunt Emily and broaden his horizons.

And, of course, there was riding. When Louis left school, his father gave him his first hunter, a young thoroughbred:

> Treat him with kindness, he said, and get to know and love him, then he will understand and trust you. What good advice that was. For the first four years after I left school that little thoroughbred and I were the very closest companions. Our greatest joy together was a day's hunting with the South Dorset or Portman hounds. He was tireless, and a wonderful stayer. Anything he could see over he would jump as boldly as a stag, but anything at all blind he seemed to feel his way over and always had a leg to spare. He never left me when we had a tumble, standing quietly but showing great impatience for me to mount again and be off. [1]

Hunting was Louis's great passion. At a time when Lord and Lady Portman followed their hounds at the head of over two hundred horsemen and horsewomen, they would ride up to twenty miles to earth or kill, and no horse-boxes for the return. It was Louis's proud claim that – except for delays from those occasional tumbles caused by hidden rabbit-holes – he was always up with the leaders.

Family tradition and this love of horsemanship led him at the age of seventeen into the Queen's Own Dorsetshire Yeomanry. Members of the Strange family had ridden with the Dorsetshires since the Regiment's formation early in the Napoleonic Wars. John Strange had joined in 1881, to become one of the Regiment's leading marksmen. The weekly training periods and the annual camp became highlights in what Louis Strange was to remember as a most happy and carefree period of his life. He enjoyed the training in scouting and in shooting. Rapid fire on advance or retirement, and mounting and dismounting at the gallop added to his skills as marksman and horseman. And how proud he was to gain third place amongst such accomplished riders in his first point-to-point with the Yeomanry. The long endurance marches and the hard living without tents and on rations of bully-beef and biscuit were but fun and games to a youth hardened by farming life and country sports. Later he would say that he owed his survival and modest achievement in two world wars to those 'fun and games': to the lessons taught and the self-discipline instilled in him by those four early years with the Yeomanry.

On special manoeuvres the Dorsetshires joined with the Yeomanry of Hampshire, Wiltshire and Somerset to form the 1st South Western Mounted Brigade. Many of those young men who rode so happily with Louis Strange across the downs and plains and through the woods and pastures of southern England were to die in North Africa, and on Chocolate Hill at Gallipoli.

In the summer of 1910, the Blandford and Wimbourne Troop, of

Louis Strange as a Trooper of the Queen's Own Dorsetshire Yeomanry at Blandford Camp in 1909.
He would rise to Sergeant then to commissioned rank in the Yeomanry

which Louis Strange was a member, was given a special task. As mounted Yeomanry, the troop was to assist the Police in controlling the crowds that were expected to swarm up to the field close to Hengistbury Head to watch the five-day Bournemouth Flying Display. It was to be the largest flying meeting yet staged in England. Flying? That sounded like fun . . .

In 1910, heavier-than-air flight was but seven years old. In Britain, it was even younger. The first flights by the American brothers, Wilbur and Orville Wright, amongst the sand-hills of Kitty Hawk, North Carolina, in 1903 had made little immediate impact, due to a surprising lack of interest amongst American newsmen and the reticence of the brothers. Such reports that did cross the Atlantic were largely disbelieved, and the aerial adventurers of Europe pursued their own individual efforts to power themselves from the ground. In Paris in 1906 the Brazilian, Alberto Santos-Dumont, became airborne in an unlikely-looking powered box-kite. Henry Farman and the Voisin brothers, amongst others, improved the design and the performance, and Louis Blériot introduced his tractor-monoplane. In 1908 the American, Samuel Cody, became the first to fly in Britain, and of more significance the Wright brothers came out of isolation to show the rest of the aviation world how to *really* fly. The demonstrations of controlled and sustained flight by Wilbur in America and by Orville in France opened up the skies. In 1909 the flight across the English

7

Channel by Louis Blériot and the first international 'air meeting' held at Reims brought the reality and potential of aviation before a world-wide audience. Public attention was grabbed again in April 1910 by the great London-to-Manchester air race between Claude Grahame-White of England and the Frenchman, Louis Paulhan, for the *Daily Mail*'s £10,000 prize. The progress of the two fliers as they tracked the railway lines towards Rugby and Crewe in their flimsy Farman biplanes was passed from signal-box to signal-box and relayed to an enthralled public by telegram and ticker-tape, by evening newspaper headlines and theatre announcements. The Frenchman won. It didn't matter. It was the daring of it and the excitement of it and the wonder of it that mattered.

It was in this aura of wonder and admiration that flying came to Bournemouth in July 1910. Louis Strange wrote of the display:

> In those days, there was a thrill in the sound of an engine being started up, another if a machine moved, and when one rose and droned round slowly in the sky, a few hundred feet over their heads, the crowds gasped with wonder and excitement, cheered the pilot to the echo when he landed, and went home thinking they had had a wonderful day's enjoyment and excitement, and enough to talk about for the rest of the year. [2]

At Bournemouth the things to be talked about were the amazing altitudes of over 4,000 feet attained by Frenchman Léon Morane in his Blériot; the daring race over the sea to the Isle of Wight's Needles and back, also won by Morane; the immaculate flying of Claude Grahame-White; the single appearance of Cody in his Flying Cathedral; the antics of the diminutive Demoiselle monoplane of bamboo and silk flown and frequently overturned by the Swiss pilot, Audemar; and the five-lap speed contests won by Captain Dickson. Sadly, most talked about of all was the death of the Honourable Charles Rolls . . .

A pioneer of aviation as well as of motoring, Charlie Rolls had gained fame as the first to achieve a double flight across the Channel. At Bournemouth, as he pulled out of a steep descent in an endeavour to land his Wright biplane 'on the spot' in the competition for landing-accuracy, he over-taxed the wooden spars that carried the tail unit. There was a sound of cracking timber. The aircraft turned onto its back and crashed to the ground from 50 feet, throwing Charlie Rolls to his death.

Flying was fun; but it was dangerous fun. Rolls was one of twenty-two fliers to die in 1910.

In the following year, Louis Strange took his first flight – as a passenger. His pilot was L W F Turner. Having learnt to fly at Grahame-White's school at Hendon, Lewis Turner had himself become an instructor of note. He had taught in Russia as chief pilot of the Kennedy Aviation School at St Petersburg before returning to England to become one of the foremost of the exhibition pilots who attracted immense crowds to the airfield at Hendon throughout the summer of 1911. He had a reputation for flying in weather conditions that would deter most aviators. When the initials L W F T appeared on the Hendon posters, it meant Lewis Will Fly Today. Lewis Turner lived at Sturminster Newton and often flew from Blandford Downs. During the summer of 1911 he took the young yeoman soldier for a 'flip' in a fragile biplane of wire-braced wood and fabric, pushed through the air by a 50-hp engine and an 8-foot-6-inch propeller. What impressed Louis Strange even more than the all-too-brief sensations of flight was the panoramic view of countryside over which he had ridden so often. But if he had thoughts at that time of becoming a pilot himself, he never spoke of it. Life was already exciting and full enough.

A year later he first encountered aircraft being used in a military role. The early involvement of the Royal Engineers in military ballooning and airship flight had led in 1911 to the formation of an Air Battalion, Royal Engineers. It was a reluctant and poorly supported step on the part of the War Office, whose general mistrust of military aviation was summed up in that same year by Sir W G Nicholson, Chief of the Imperial General Staff. 'Aviation,' he said, 'is a useless and expensive fad advocated by a few individuals whose ideas are unworthy of attention.'

The formation in 1912 of a Royal Flying Corps (RFC) was another step forward, but it attracted little material backing. For the autumn manoeuvres of 1912 the RFC could muster only fourteen flimsy biplanes and three airships. The sole purpose of this force was reconnaissance in direct support of the ground battle, a role in which it achieved moderate success. The potential of aerial observation certainly impressed one young cavalryman – Louis Strange. Serving with the Yeomanry in those manoeuvres, he was on a scouting patrol when a plane flew over. Reining in his mount to watch the majestic and unimpeded progress of the machine above him, he recalled the wide-reaching view that he himself had enjoyed from such a seat in the sky during his flight with Lewis Turner. How much easier it would be, he thought, to plot enemy dispositions and movements from an aeroplane: easier than from the saddle of a horse.

It was not until the following year that he voiced that thought. He was at the May 1913 training camp with the Dorsetshires. A glass or two of wine had been taken with dinner, and a few more to follow. Conversation was boisterous. It turned to the topic of military strategies. Some were for change, most were against it. Louis, already a forward-thinker and innovator, spoke loudly for the minority. Britain, he said – perhaps, recalling opinions that he had read in newspapers, in particular in the *Daily Mail* – had ceased to be an island the day that Blériot had flown the Channel. The aeroplane would be a major weapon in any future war. Why, he said, warming to his theme, it would even replace the cavalry as a means of military reconnaissance.

Uproar! What a declaration to make amongst the horsemen of the Yeomanry! Their fathers and their fathers' fathers had ridden to war, and so would they! Aeroplanes indeed! Amongst the riot of dissension a voice hotly suggested that if young Strange thought so highly of these infernal machines, why didn't he learn to fly one?

'I will!' declared 'young Strange', just as hotly. 'The first chance I get, I'll learn to fly. What's more, I'll wager that next year I will fly over camp – just to prove it!'

'You're on! You're on!' cried several voices.

How many adventures are undertaken at such moments, perhaps to be regretted in the more sober light of morning? Louis admitted that it had been a rash vow, but having made that promise, he was determined to keep it at the first opportunity. Opportunity, however, was a rare thing in a farmer's summer. It is likely that had fate not intervened, the summer of 1913 would have passed without offering him a chance to leave the farm for more than a few days at a time. Then it would have been winter; not a season in which to learn to fly the fragile machines of the day. And 1914 would have brought new priorities as the world slid towards conflict.

But fate did intervene. It came that July in the form of a ewe that was suffering from footrot. As Louis was endeavouring to treat the animal, it delivered him a hefty kick in the ribs. The damage to the young man was severe enough to put a temporary end to his practical usefulness on the farm, but he would still be capable, he supposed, of handling the simple controls of an aeroplane.

He hunted up Lewis Turner. If he could make himself available at Hendon for a few weeks, would Lewis teach him to fly? Gladly, said Lewis Turner. So Louis Strange went flying. All because of a sheep with footrot.

CHAPTER TWO

Ragtime Flying

When Louis Strange went to Hendon to learn to fly in 1913, this aerodrome on the northern fringe of London had become Britain's most popular aviation centre. In 1910 Louis Paulhan had used the field for the start of his race to Manchester against Claude Grahame-White, who had subsequently bought the land. Under the energetic supervision of his general manager, Richard Gates, the pastures over which Louis Strange's mother had once looked from her window in Hydemoor House had been cleared, drained and levelled to create an oval airfield 2 miles in circumference. Seven 'sheds' had been built to house the Grahame-White Aviation Company and its flying-school. Assistant Manager Bernard Isaacs had launched an effective publicity campaign and had also attracted commercial sponsorship for races and other forms of aerial competition. In this heroic age of British aviation, the weekend crowds had flocked from London to watch the pylon races and the exhibitions of 'crazy flying'; to see the latest types of flying-machine and the foremost aviators of the day; and to venture into the air themselves as paying passengers.

By 1913, a large public enclosure, a restaurant, a hotel and more sheds had been added. Passengers, now averaging a hundred a week, were no longer content with a circuit of the airfield. For £10 they could now fly to Elstree and back. For £26 they could take a 38-mile return flight to Brooklands, another of Britain's pioneer airfields. To cater for this 'joy-riding', Grahame-White had produced his Aerobus to carry five passengers in an elongated nacelle. Shortly after Louis Strange arrived, the millionth spectator passed through the airfield's turnstiles. 'London's Modern Rendezvous' was the name they gave to Hendon in 1913.

The young farmer took rooms in Colindale Avenue. One of the first things that he learnt about flying was that it involved early rising. Although the days were gone when most pilots would puff cigarette smoke into the air then go back inside the shed if it wavered too far from the perpendicular, learning to fly was still best done in the calm airs of dawn. Early mornings, however, offered no hardship to a dairy farmer. His cheery greetings attracted bleary groans from other aviators.

Lewis Turner was instructing for the Ewen School, one of several that had joined Grahame-White at Hendon. In fact, Louis Strange received most of his instruction from the Swiss aviator, Édouard Baumann, whose opening exhortation to trainees was, 'It is not for pupils to forget what I say.' He would then wave an arm towards the hangar which housed the remnants of several crashed machines before adding, 'You see I have already too much work of forgetfulness in that shed there.' [1]

Louis Strange was taught to fly on a Caudron tractor biplane powered by a 35-hp Anzani engine. It had no dual control: no such luxury existed in 1913. He began his training seated at the controls of the aeroplane mounted on two trestles. He was shown how to manipulate the 'stick' that operated the elevator and ailerons, and the foot-bar to control the rudder. The required angles of the aeroplane in relation to the ground at various stages of take-off, flight and landing were simulated by adjustments to the trestles. Baumann then took his pupil for a series of short flights to accustom him to the sensations and to train his eye in the judgement of height, distance and the angle of approach for that all-important landing. 'Any fool can fly, but it takes a pilot to land,' was an apt judgement of the era. Huddled behind his instructor on an open seat amongst the maze of bracing wires and in the whip of the 50-mph airstream, with his cap turned back-to-front in approved fashion, Louis was allowed to reach round and place his hand over Baumann's to feel the sure but never-hasty manipulation of the control stick.

When the Swiss flier was satisfied that the likelihood of young Strange turning the Caudron onto its back had diminished to an acceptable level, Louis was allowed to 'roll' the aircraft to and fro across the field. When he had ironed the zigzags out of this progress and could maintain a straight course with the tail raised from the ground, he advanced to short hops into the air. Distance was added, but the brief flights were still in straight lines; or reasonably straight lines. Any necessary corrections to technique were practised back on the trestles. Wisely, instructors rarely accompanied their pupils on these first ventures from the ground. When Louis could fly the length of the aerodrome, altitude was increased, and the first turns attempted – initially to the left because the revolution of the propeller encouraged the machine in that direction, then to the right. When turns in both directions had been mastered, they were alternated in figures-of-eight, to and fro across the field. These would be the basis of the proficiency test. Landings with the engine cut, to bring the brakeless aeroplane to rest in approximately the required spot, demanded much practice.

Training was not constant. It required the coincidental presence of Baumann, the Caudron and favourable weather. But Louis Strange was an apt pupil. It was believed in the early days of powered flight that there was a close correlation between horsemanship and airmanship. Both needed courage and spirit. Both benefited from an eye for speed and distance; from a seat-of-the-pants feel for movement and an automatic response to it; from a firm but gentle hand on the 'controls'. It was not long before Louis Strange was riding through the air with the same surety and panache that he showed when riding to hounds. After three weeks at Hendon and three and a half hours actually in the air, he was declared fit to attempt the series of manoeuvres that – if the engine held out long enough – would gain him his certificate of proficiency from the Royal Aero Club.

On 5th August, in the presence of two official observers, Louis Strange made the required two flights, each of 5 kilometres, weaving his figures-of-eight to and fro across the aerodrome at a height of some 300 feet, and on both occasions putting the Caudron down with engine stopped, and rolling it to rest well within the required 50 metres from the chosen spot. He was awarded Royal Aero Club Certificate No. 575. He was a pilot.

Louis Strange returned to his farm at Lower Almer. But he left his heart at Hendon. It was still flying figures-of-eight through the wind-whip at 300 feet, still gliding down to the grass with the motor cut and just the music of wind in the wires. Louis Strange would never lose his love of the land. Throughout his life he would periodically return to it, and when necessary would take comfort from it. But now a new love called. Flying had captivated him.

He could not afford to buy and maintain his own aeroplane, but continue to fly he must. Even before he left Hendon he had submitted an application for a commission in the Royal Flying Corps (RFC) Reserve. He had no thought at that time of joining the Regular service, but if he could transfer from the Yeomanry to the RFC Reserve, his annual training would be spent flying instead of riding, which he could do at any time. But the prospect of flying for just three weeks in the year was not enough. He was soon back at Hendon. Just for the weekend. Then for another weekend. The French aviator, Louis Noel, taught him to fly the Grahame-White Box-Kite. Claude Grahame-White himself was impressed at the speed and enthusiasm with which the young pilot progressed. Would Strange like to fly for him? He could take passengers for 'flips', and fly in the weekend races and exhibitions. He could become an instructor for the Grahame-White School. He wouldn't be paid much, but he would get plenty of flying, at little expense to himself. What did he think?

Louis Strange won his first aerial race in this Grahame-White Box-Kite biplane in August 1913

Louis thought it was an opportunity not to be missed. But he could not farm Lower Almer *and* become a professional pilot. He would have to give up the farm. John Strange, rightly fearful of this venture and firm in his belief that the place of a Strange was on the land, not in the sky, tried to dissuade his son from such rashness. But Louis had inherited his father's strong will and fierce independence, and his new love tugged at him.

So Louis Strange left the farm at Lower Almer, took permanent rooms at Hendon, and flew.

He flew whenever he could and whatever he could: the Grahame-White Box-Kite, the Caudron, the Morane, the Blériot monoplane, the Henry Farman. During the week he gave instruction to others. At weekends he took paying customers for flights, and took part in aerial displays and races. In August he won his first cross-country race – to Mill Hill and back in the Grahame-White biplane. In September he came first in a pylon race. In October he noted that he 'Instructed 22 pupils and took up 15 passengers'. One of those passengers was an attractive girl called Marjorie, who would later become his wife.

By the end of 1913 Louis Strange was established as one of Hendon's regular fliers. These pioneers of British exhibition flying were as well known to the London audiences as were the foremost sportsmen and actors of the day. There were the Americans, Beatty and Brock; Louis Noel, Verrier, Marty and Desoutter from France; Baumann of Switzerland; Spratt the South African; and the British fliers, Manton, Carr, Goodden, Birchenough, Hucks, Richard Gates,

14

Lewis Turner, Gustav Hamel and of course Claude Grahame-White himself. Louis Strange also met the frequent and famed visitors from the other flying-centres of Eastchurch and Brooklands, from the Royal Aero Club and from the youthful aviation industry. In such company his education in flying was thorough and rapid. When these enthusiasts of the first decade of powered flight were not actually flying, they were discussing it, arguing about it. Flying was still an imprecise art. There was much debate over still-unresolved principles of flight: angles of incidence, centres of gravity, stability, wing-loading. There were discussions about the handling and gliding characteristics of different types of aircraft. There were arguments over the relative merits of tractors and pushers, of monoplanes and biplanes. There was so much yet unknown, and only one way to find out: try it. If it didn't work, put the pieces together, go up and try again.

They were exciting times.

The spirit of these youthful pioneers found expression not only in the sky, but also on the ground. In January of 1914 they held their famous 'Upside Down Dinner'. It was all to do with looping the loop . . .

The Frenchman, Adolphe Pégoud, had been acclaimed as the first to achieve what was seen as an extraordinary feat when on 21st September 1913 he looped a specially strengthened Blériot mono-

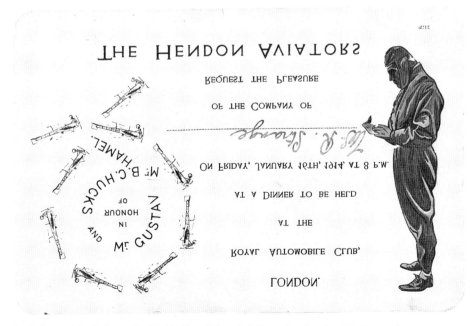

Louis Strange's invitation to the 'Upside Down Dinner', deliberately printed upside-down and back-to-front

plane. Later he introduced a roll into level flight off the top of the loop – a manoeuvre to be reintroduced for more deadly purpose by the German fighter ace, Max Immelman. Shortly after Pégoud had shown the way, Benfield Charles Hucks had become the first Englishman to loop and to fly intentionally inverted – at Buc in France – also in a strengthened machine. Louis Strange had been amongst the party of Hendon fliers who had met Hucks at Charing Cross to carry him in triumph from the station – upside-down, of course. Then Gustav Hamel had looped at Hendon in a standard Morane and had repeated the feat with a passenger, the very daring Miss Trehawke Davies, with her skirts tightly secured. It was to celebrate the looping by Hucks and Hamel that the Hendon fliers staged the 'Upside Down Dinner' at the Royal Automobile Club's premises in Pall Mall on 16th January 1914.

Tables were arranged in the pattern of a loop, with upside-down tables placed on top of normal ones, and an upside-down figure in an upside-down fuselage suspended above. The meal itself was also 'upside-down'. It began with coffee, liqueurs and cigars, followed by a sweet, then the main course of *Bécassines à la Hamel* – snipe. Then came lobster, which in the deft hands of waiters dressed in mechanics' overalls, performed a series of perfect loops before being served. After soup came the hors-d'oeuvre to end this topsy-turvy dinner. Hucks endeavoured to drink champagne from an inverted glass and Charles Coburn sang 'Two Lovely Black Eyes' standing on his head. Claude Grahame-White, as chairman, greeted the prestigious guests from the aviation world as they left.

Shortly afterwards, to the delight of the Hendon crowd, five more pilots added their names to the list of inverted fliers. First Carr went over the top, and later on the same day Goodden, Louis Strange, Hall and Louis Noel followed suit. There was, for a while, a mania for looping. There were few other aerobatics at that time. Steep ascents and near-vertical dives; slow flying to the point of progressing backwards in a strong head wind; steep banking on the turns; 'bombing' competitions and target landings, and particularly the pylon and cross-country races – these were the ingredients of an air display in early 1914. 'Ragtime flying' it had been christened by Richard Gates. Now looping and inverted flight were added to the menu.

Although a relative newcomer to the Hendon fliers, by the time of the five-day Easter Show in 1914 Louis Strange was making his mark amongst them. In particular he was gaining a reputation as a cross-country racer. He won the 17-mile race at the Hendon March Meeting, beating his old instructor Louis Noel into second place. In

REGINALD H. CARR

F.W. GOODDEN

J.L.HALL.

L.A.STRANGE

LOUIS NOEL.

FLIGHT.

THE FIVE PILOTS WHO, AT HENDON AERODROME, EACH FOR THE FIRST TIME LOOPED THE LOOP ON WEDNESDAY LAST WEEK.

Shortly after the 'Upside Down Dinner', five other British pilots – including Louis Strange (bottom left) – became 'loopers'. (Flight, *4th April 1914*)

that year's 'Aerial Derby' – a 94-mile circuit of London – he was flying well in atrocious visibility when a faulty petrol-pump forced him down at West Wickham. On 20th June, he was one of eight starters in the prestigious London–Manchester–London Air Race. Flying a Blériot monoplane with an 80-hp Gnome engine, he led the race into Manchester, thirty-five minutes ahead of his closest rival, Brock. Over 100,000 people flocked to Trafford Park to see the fliers arrive. In its

For the *Daily Mail*'s London–
Manchester–London race in
1914, Louis Strange flew this
Blériot X1-2 monoplane

description of the event, the *Daily Mail* – main sponsor of the race and
several streets ahead of the Government in its support for British
aviation – painted this picture of Edwardian society and the spirit with
which it greeted the marvel of powered flight:

> Dignified city men lolled on the grass, drank ginger beer and ate
> sandwiches like happy schoolboys. The parasols, white dresses, and
> dainty hats of the womenfolk made the enclosure look particularly
> bright. Along the road near by were coco-nut shies, ice-cream stalls,
> political speakers and purveyors of medicine for almost all the ailments
> known to man.
>
> All Manchester seemed to be at Trafford Park, and at 1.33 all
> Manchester seemed to gasp slightly – the visible expression of a new
> sensation. 'One's coming,' everyone whispered or shouted according to
> temperament.
>
> Away in the south was a tiny speck. Almost immediately it grew into
> the graceful shape and proportion of the sleek, racy-looking monoplane.

18

Mr L A Strange was the first to arrive at the Manchester control. He received a magnificent welcome, not the least part of which was that accorded to him by the Lord Mayor of Manchester . . . [2]

Unfortunately, the Lord Mayor of Manchester, Alderman McCabe, was a portly gentleman. In his enthusiasm to be the first to shake the hand of the intrepid flier, he used the undercarriage bracing wires as a ladder. When Louis Strange took off from the field for the return leg of a race that was surely his, the over-taxed fitting snapped, the bracing wire flew into the propeller, and the propeller flew into pieces. Louis Strange was out of the race.

Brock took the *Daily Mail* Gold Trophy and £650 in prize-money. Louis blamed nobody but himself. He would always hold that practically every flying accident was the fault of the pilot, whose responsibility extended to the maintenance and checking of his own machine. In fact he was one of very few pilots in the first decade of powered flight who could claim never to have crashed an aeroplane in over a hundred hours of flying. As a passenger, however, he experienced the sensations of aerial disaster. It happened at Hendon . . .

A very strong, gusty wind was blowing that day, so that there seemed little chance of carrying out the flying programme, but as a large crowd

Leading the race at the halfway stage, Louis is greeted at Manchester by the Lord Mayor, Alderman McCabe

19

London-Manchester-London.   TIME CARD.

No. **6**   Name of Competitor *L. A. Strange*

Machine *Bleriot Monoplane 80 H.P. Gnome Engine*

OUTWARD.	Time of Arrival.			Depart.			Signature of Timekeeper.
HENDON Start				10	28	48	*A.m/*
BIRMINGHAM	12	7	49	12	37	49	*A.W.*
MANCHESTER	1	36	30	2	36	30	*C.F.Y.*
HOMEWARD. MANCHESTER	1	36	30	2	36	30	*C.F.Y.*
BIRMINGHAM							
HENDON							

Louis Strange's time card for the race was never completed: his aircraft failed on taking off from Manchester

had assembled, it was obvious that something had to be done. The first machine to be brought out was an 80-hp Morane monoplane, piloted by Philip Marty, who asked me if I would like to accompany him as passenger. With the enthusiasm of youth I agreed to do so; but it was not long before I had cause to regret my rashness.

Marty taxied out to the far side of the aerodrome in order to take off into the wind; but the machine left the ground all too quickly, with the result that a strong gust lifted us up about 40 feet in the air and then left us in a stalled attitude, with practically no forward speed. The machine staggered for an ominous moment and then stalled. I have never forgotten the horrible sensations of the next few seconds. The left wing seemed to drop out of sight, and I saw the right wing sweep round the sky above us like a sort of windmill vane. Then the roar of the engine stopped.

20

I thanked heaven that Marty switched off in time, for a second later the Morane's nose hit the ground with a bang and a crash. As she cartwheeled over on to her back, I ducked well down inside the fuselage, and there we were – upside-down, unable to move an inch and fairly soaked with petrol from the burst tank. Miraculously as it may seem, I was entirely unhurt, while Marty came off equally well except that he caught his head between the top longeron of the machine and the ground, which, luckily for him, formed a slight hollow at that spot. He kept on yelling something in French, which I did not understand.

I could not help laughing, which drew from him a torrent of mingled English and French profanity, which sounded so funny that I went on laughing. Meanwhile the aerodrome staff had hastened to the scene of disaster. When the machine's tail was lifted up, we both fell out of the fuselage, whereupon all our rescuers began to laugh. This only sent Marty off into further spasms of mirth-provoking Anglo-French fury . . . [1]

Although the crumpling of spars and fabric cushioned many such accidents, not all of them ended in laughter. Two weeks later, Philip Marty stalled again while giving a slow-flying exhibition. He crashed from no more than 200 feet. This time he died in the wreckage. Earlier that year Louis Strange had heard the engine of Lee Temple's Blériot suddenly stop in level flight and had watched the monoplane pitch forward into an involuntary bunt, to land on its back in the middle of the airfield, killing its pilot outright. And at the time that Marty died, there was Desoutter hobbling back to Hendon on the artificial leg that had replaced the one sliced off in a crash the previous autumn, determined still to fly. Offered a cumbersome wooden leg, Desoutter had decided to redesign his own anatomy, and had produced a limb of aluminium. He patented his invention which, sadly, was to be much in demand during the years 1914–18. Then in May the great Gustav Hamel was lost. He took off from close to Boulogne to fly to Hendon and was never seen again. It was presumed that he had crashed at sea. Other pilots grieved the loss of good friends, learned what they could from the accidents, and went on flying.

In addition to his growing prowess as a racing pilot, Louis Strange was also coming to the fore in the aerial bombing contests. His first victory was at Hendon on the 1st of May, with an average distance of 25 feet 3 inches from target centre for two bags of flour dropped from 300 feet. Grahame-White had imported this event from the USA, where amongst his considerable triumphs over American fliers in 1910, he had won a bombing contest at the Boston/Harvard meet. He had introduced the event at Hendon and during the flying shows that he gave throughout southern England in 1911 – not only as an attraction but as part of his campaign to alert Members of Parliament and the public to the potential of aerial warfare and Britain's unpreparedness for it. Few had taken note.

Louis Strange's success in pitching dummy bombs onto a variety of ground targets was a sadly prophetic omen. By mid-1914 Europe was rumbling towards war on a massive scale. With equal inevitability, Louis Strange was being borne towards the conflict, on fragile wings of fabric and wood.

Shortly after he had submitted his application to join the Royal Flying Corps (RFC), Louis Strange had been summoned for interview at the War Office. He was seen by Major Sefton Brancker, who was to become Major General Sir Sefton Brancker, and whose subsequent career as an energetic Director of Civil Aviation would later be cut short by his death in the ill-fated airship R101.

Louis Strange appeared to have all the right qualifications for an officer of the RFC, thought Sefton Brancker. He had been to a good school, was a keen sportsman and a riding man. Damn it – the fellow could actually fly!

Louis Strange was told that his application would be favourably considered, and that he was to await instructions as to the time and place of his course of Army aviation training. The call did not come until May 1914, when he was ordered to attend No. Six Course of instruction at the Central Flying School (CFS), at Upavon in Wiltshire.

The CFS had been formed in 1912. Its purpose was not the basic training of pilots. Neither the Army nor the Royal Navy could afford that. The role of CFS was to convert fliers who already held the Royal Aero Club ticket into military aviators. Those few regular officers who saw military potential in flight had been required to pay their way through flying training at centres such as Hendon and Brooklands before undertaking a course in military aviation. If accepted by the RFC they received a refund of £75 towards those costs. Others, like Louis Strange, came into the RFC primarily to pursue their love of flying. The system, as well as being kind to military funding, ensured that applicants were of the 'right' type: men of spirit and of means.

Louis Strange sent a copy of his orders to the Adjutant of the Dorsetshire Yeomanry to explain his forthcoming absence from that year's camp. He still belonged to the Dorsetshires, for officers and other ranks of the RFC and the Royal Naval Air Service (RNAS) were only attached to this new military arm from their Regiments or ships.

The Commandant of CFS was Captain Godfrey Paine of the Royal

Navy, known as 'Bloody Paine' from his mastery of invective, soon to be directed at Louis Strange. The Assistant Commandant was Major Trenchard. Within two years Lieutenant Strange would be stepping into Trenchard's shoes, while Trenchard himself would rise to the command of an independent Royal Air Force.

Louis Strange had kept no record of his flying at Hendon. The flying was what mattered, not writing about it. His first log-book, maintained none-too-tidily in a plain Army exercise book (Army Book 130), notes that his first flight at CFS was at 0730 on 14th May 1914, in a Henry Farman under the instruction of Major Gerrard. There were three more brief flights that same evening. On the second of them he had been allowed to fly solo, for although nobody was going to admit it, it was already apparent that young Lieutenant Strange was a better flier than most of his instructors. He was still required, however, to follow the requisite progressions, and never would be allowed to demonstrate his repertoire of ragtime flying.

Flying at CFS in 1914 was unadventurous. Most flights took place in the early morning and late afternoon, when the winds of Salisbury Plain were kind to aeroplanes. Gentle circuits of the aerodrome, progressing to longer cross-country routes at constant altitude and in level flight, were all that were required of the military pilot. Violent manoeuvre was discouraged. Stunting was positively forbidden. Not only might it tear the wings off the machine; military flying foresaw no need for vigorous diversion from the straight and level. The role of the aeroplane in war was to provide an aerial observation platform. Stability and not getting lost too often were all that were required of the military pilot, not fancy flying. The aerobatic contortions of the dogfight lay in a future foreseen by very few.

Louis Strange was made acutely aware of the official view of stunting on the day that the fuel-pipe of the Blériot he was piloting above Upavon broke, spraying him with petrol from the service-tank close to his face. Sensing that he was losing consciousness from the fumes, he threw the plane into a fierce side-slip to divert the stream of petrol and to bathe himself in a rush of clean air. With the skill of a ragtime flier, he side-slipped the Blériot down from 5,000 feet until he was low enough to switch off the engine and flatten out for landing:

> That meant that I got the full force of the petrol fumes again, and although I held my breath as long as possible, I was completely gassed once more. Somehow or other I managed to put her down safely, and naturally did not worry about the fact that I had landed her some 200 yards away from the tarmac, another thing we had been told never to do. The other was side-slipping . . .

Louis Strange flew the Blériot both as a civilian and as a military pilot

Capt. Godfrey Paine, who was on the tarmac, came along to see what was the matter. Instead of receiving the pat on the back I might have felt I deserved for bringing myself and my machine safely down, I had to listen to a wonderful flow of language, in which the profanity of land, sea and air was beautifully mingled. As the Commandant was a master of his art, and I was hardly more than semi-conscious at the time, I rather enjoyed listening to the rich variety of his lurid vocabulary, until at last my wits returned. Then I realised that I was the unfortunate object of his heartfelt curses and that he thought I had been stunting on purpose. At last, however, he gave me a chance to offer my explanation, and as the state of my clothing, which was soaked with petrol, substantiated my tale, he calmed down and was quite nice to me, which was as it should be. [1]

Louis Strange was frustrated by the restrictions placed on his flying, and took what opportunity he could to rebel against them – always out of sight, of course. Hidden from official eyes by convenient cloud or high ground, or better still by sheer distance, he would indulge in a little ragtime flying of his own. It was an early indication of a disdain of military dogmatism and red tape that would accompany him throughout his Service career. And when he was not required to spend his weekends at Upavon, he would hurry back to Hendon, to do some *real* flying for the crowds. The Service gave him special dispensation to fly in the Aerial Derby and the Manchester race.

At the end of May he was able to claim on his wager of the

previous year. The Dorsetshire Yeomanry were training at Crichel Park. It was a triumphant 'young Strange' who flew over their lines, to the great consternation of the horses, then landed to collect his bets. Permitted now to range wider on his cross-country flights, he also managed several 'forced landings' close to his own home and to those of friends. On one occasion he overstayed his visiting. Flares had to be lit on the aerodrome at Upavon to light his return, and he received another dressing-down. Flying in the dark was also forbidden.

After showing his mastery of the Henry Farman, he was advanced to the BE-2a and the BE-8, under the guidance of Captain Conran. The BE series were tractor biplanes, designed by Geoffrey De Havilland on Blériot lines (BE stood for Blériot Experimental) and produced at the Royal Aircraft Factory at Farnborough. The BE-2a was a relatively stable aircraft, with a 70-hp Renault engine that could power it to over 60 mph. The BE-8 offered the novelty of a double cockpit, which Louis found gave just enough space for two men to get admirably in each other's way.

There was great excitement on Salisbury Plain in June when the entire Military Wing of the RFC assembled in a tented camp at Netheravon for a month of combined training. Whenever weather permitted, an assortment of aeroplanes buzzed to and fro above the Plain with the sound of demented sewing-machines. Of the seventy aircraft that were gathered there, many were of French origin or derivation, with French engines. Almost all were biplanes. A spate of well publicised accidents in monoplanes during 1912 and 1913 had brought official condemnation upon the single wing. None of the RFC machines had been designed specifically for aerial warfare. They were basically 'sporting' aeroplanes, just as most of their pilots were converted 'sporting' fliers. However, the fact that the planes were not designed to carry either offensive or defensive weapons was not seen as a cause for concern, as their sole purpose remained that of reconnaissance in support of ground operations. How this reconnaissance was to be carried out and how the information gained was to be communicated to the ground forces had not yet been firmly established. It remained a matter for individual and Squadron initiative rather than standard procedure. Even this limited role had few supporters amongst the prospective commanders of those ground forces. Sir Douglas Haig, speaking to senior officers as Commander-in-Chief Aldershot in July said, 'I hope none of you gentlemen is so foolish as to think that aeroplanes will be usefully employed for reconnaissance in the air. There is only one way for a commander to get information by reconnaissance and that is by the use of cavalry.'

Fortunately, that small band of pioneer military aviators gathered at Netheravon and those soon to join their ranks from across the valley at Upavon thought otherwise.

During his 10 weeks at CFS Louis Strange had flown 52 hours. No. Six Course was in the final stages of its training. Examinations were in the offing, and nobody was looking forward to them. War was rumoured, of course, and much discussed, but few really believed that it would happen. If it did, it would be brief and glorious . . .

Then came the morning towards the end of July when the trainees responded as usual to their dawn *réveille* – to find that flying had been cancelled. They were told that all the CFS aircraft had been withdrawn from training and were being prepared for active service. Later that day they were called together to be addressed by Captain Paine. He told them that war with Germany was imminent; that they would no doubt be delighted to hear that examinations were cancelled; and that those who were considered to be proficient would be posted to Active Service Squadrons forthwith. There was much excitement. War! Much better than having to sit exams. The only ones who were unhappy were those considered not yet skilled enough to take on the Hun. If they didn't get to grips with him at the outset, it would all be over, they feared.

Louis Strange was amongst the proficient. He packed his kit, and the following day reported to the RFC Headquarters at Farnborough. From there he was promptly despatched to Gosport, with orders to join No. 5 Squadron, being prepared for service in France should it become necessary.

It became necessary on 4th August, the day on which war against Germany was declared. The ragtime flying was over.

CHAPTER THREE

The First War in the Air

When Europe went to war in 1914 it took its fledgling air forces with it, although it wasn't quite sure what to do with them.

Britain had the least well equipped of the major combatant air forces. It could muster 113 aircraft, most of them French, and 6 airships, and had little domestic capacity for adding to these numbers in the short term. The parlous state of the British aircraft industry was not due to any lack of enthusiasm and ability amongst potential manufacturers. The pioneers of that industry, such as Roe, Sopwith, Handley Page and Grahame-White, had been starved of encouragement and funds by a government whose meagre subsidy was concentrated on the Royal Aircraft Factory at Farnborough.

Reconnaissance remained the primary – and in the opinions of most, the only – military task for the aeroplane. Some commanders had recognised bombing and artillery co-operation as potential roles, but none of the air forces now flexing their fabric wings had given serious thought to shooting each other out of the sky. The foresight of such individuals as Major Brooke-Popham, who recommended mounting weapons on aeroplanes as early as 1910, was largely ignored. No – it was generally considered that if the aeroplane was to serve any military purpose at all, it would be as an aerial scout: an eye in the sky. For this of course, it would be required to fly straight and level, at about 2,000 feet. Nor, if further argument against an offensive role was needed, could the poorly powered machines of 1914 struggle into the air with much in the way of weaponry. As Louis Strange was soon to discover . . .

He joined No. 5 Squadron at Gosport in time to help with the frantic preparations for a possible movement to France. During brief moments of relaxation in the squadron quarters in Fort Grange, the men of No. 5 Squadron listened to the transports going down the Solent, bearing the five Divisions of the British Expeditionary Force (BEF) across the Channel. Would the four operational squadrons of the RFC be going with them? The young fliers of No. 5 certainly hoped so. It would all be over by Christmas. They didn't want to miss the fun. They shared the nationalistic fervour that gripped most of Europe, that was dragging it into a war of unforeseen consequences, aided by complex defence treaties and mobilisation plans that once set in motion seemed unstoppable.

After several days of impatience and speculation the order came: Nos 2, 3, 4 and 5 Squadrons of the RFC were to cross the Channel and form at Amiens, to support the BEF. Within the hour, No. 5 Squadron's column of support vehicles rolled out of Fort Grange for Southampton docks. They were as motley a collection of civilian machines as were the aeroplanes that would hopefully follow them across the water. The Squadron's 'bomb lorry' still advertised Lazenby's Sauce. Also represented were Carter Paterson, Peak Frean Biscuits and Bovril, the latter emblazoned on a bright red background that was soon to provide a valuable landmark for fliers lost above the unfamiliar fields of France and Flanders.

On the following day, 14th August 1914, the aeroplanes of the four RFC Squadrons congregated at Dover. At least, most of them did. Four of the No. 5 Squadron pilots and several from other squadrons either crashed or force-landed on the way there, without serious injury except to Lieutenant Skene and Air Mechanic Barlow of No. 3 Squadron, who died when their plane crashed shortly after take-off from Netheravon. Nobody considered the toll exceptional. Those who reached Dover landed to the rapturous applause of the populace gathered on the cliff-top meadows, close to where Louis Blériot had touched down just five years earlier. Now, in aircraft little improved since then, the pilots of the RFC faced the same perilous crossing. After being fêted that night by the folk of Dover, they took off in ones and twos early the next morning, and headed for France and the first war in the air. There were thirty-seven of them. Only seven of those pioneers of aerial combat would survive the war.

Louis Strange was one of the last to leave Dover. With Air Mechanic Walls of the Squadron's mechanical transport section as passenger, and the only one to burden his aircraft with a Lewis gun, he had left Gosport in Henry Farman F-20 No. 341 at 6 a.m. on 14th August:

> Well, we started off all right; but I soon saw that my machine would require careful handling if we were to avoid coming to grief, because my passenger weighed thirteen stone, while in addition to my own kit (and Lewis gun) I had to carry his kit and rifle. My load was far too heavy for safety, but having had experience with 35-hp Blériots, I knew how to manage a machine that would only just fly.
>
> We struggled on to Shoreham where we landed to fill up with petrol. To add to our troubles there was a strong wind against us. As crows are supposed to fly it is about seventy-odd miles to Dover, but it took me two

and a half hours to get there, while at one time I had hard work to avoid being battered down on to the Sussex Downs.

At Dover I found that the aerodrome lay on high ground at the edge of the cliffs above the Castle. There were a number of red flags, which told me of ditches to be avoided, but whether the supply of flags had run short or whether some careless fellow had left a ditch unmarked through negligence, I cannot tell; the main thing is that after landing safely, I ran into an unmarked ditch and broke a longeron.

Before I could see what I was going to do about it, I had to attend to the troubles of my passenger, who had contrived to smuggle a bottle of whiskey with him. Having emptied its contents *en route*, he threw it overboard when we reached Dover, but the combined effects of the alcohol and his first flight were such that I found it necessary to place him under arrest.

After seeing him shipped off to the guard tent, I had some tea at the Castle. I then set off for Farnborough in a Rolls Royce to get a new longeron. I reached Dover again at 2 a.m. and worked till 6 a.m., removing the broken longeron and replacing it with the new one.

I now thought I was ready to start. Having got some breakfast in the Castle, I returned to the aerodrome, where I found that the transport driver had escaped from the guard tent and could not be found. It was not until 10.30 that the police rounded him up somewhere in Dover, still very much the worse for drink . . . I did not leave the white cliffs of Old England until the disgracefully late hour of 12 noon on Sunday, August 16th.

The sea below me was rough, and my crossing to Gris Nez took a long forty-five minutes. I had some worried moments over the water. As the visibility was not more than about half a mile, I began to wonder if I was not running up alongside the coast of Belgium. Suddenly the visibility became even worse, and when I eventually sighted the grey cliffs of Gris Nez they were only a few hundred yards away. But a sharp right hand bank took me clear of the cliff, and then I hugged the coastline down to Boulogne, where I ran into better weather. Although I encountered a couple of hard rainstorms later, I was able to make Amiens comfortably in about two and a half hours flying time.

I shall never forget taxiing up to the other machines that Sunday afternoon. The thousands of Frenchmen congregated round the aerodrome at Amiens put me in mind of a Hendon pageant, but the illusion vanished when the machine came to a standstill because, much to my astonishment, my passenger stood up and answered the cheers of the crowd with much gusto and saluted the Entente Cordiale by waving aloft another empty bottle of whiskey. At that moment my eye caught that of Major Higgins, my commanding officer . . . [1]

Air Mechanic Walls received fifty-six days No. 1 Field Punishment, and Lieutenant Strange was roundly ticked off by his Squadron Commander. However, as he said:

> I was a good deal luckier than Lieutenant Vaughan. He had a forced landing near Boulogne, where French villagers made up their minds that he was a German airman, and as nothing he could say convinced them to the contrary, they clapped him in the local gaol, where he had to kick his heels for three days before he was released. [1]

And Lieutenant Vaughan was luckier than Lieutenant Copland Perry, killed when he crashed near Amiens in a BE-8 – 'a short lived nasty contraption with insufficient fin surface' said Louis Strange's Flight Commander, Captain Carmichael, who also flew a BE-8 across the Channel. [2]

And so the Royal Flying Corps came to France in 1914.

Germany's strategic plan at the outbreak of war was simple. Feeling itself threatened by Russia to the east and by France to the west, it sought to strike hard at France with a massive right hook through a militarily inept Belgium; defeat the French 'before leaf-fall'; then turn its full military force against Russia. It was the unprovoked invasion of Belgium that brought Britain, through treaty, into the war, brought the BEF into position on the left flank of the French armies and brought the RFC to Amiens to support it.

Louis Strange's first duty was to attend the funerals of Copland Perry and the mechanic who had died with him. All four Squadrons of the RFC then took up position at Maubeuge. Louis's close friend Robert Smith Barry crashed on the way, shattering his leg and killing his passenger. This wouldn't stop Smith Barry from becoming, like Louis Strange, one of the great innovators of the early years of aerial warfare.

A few tentative sorties were flown from Maubeuge, and there was much excitement when a Blériot of No. 2 Squadron returned with twelve bullet-holes in its fabric and one in the backside of its observer, Sergeant Major Jillings. The bullets had been French, not German, it was thought. Mostly the fliers sat in fine sunshine listening to distant rumbles that could have been thunder but in fact came from the German bombardment of the Liège forts. They also listened with pride and confidence to the infantry marching past the aerodrome to the stirring ring of their regimental bands as the BEF moved up to Mons.

On 22nd August, after less than a week in France, Louis Strange and other pilots were alerted by excited shouts. A German aircraft was

Lieutenant L A Strange of the Royal Flying Corps was one of the first thirty-seven pilots to fly across the Channel to begin the air war against Germany in 1914 (*Photo: Chaz Bowyer*)

flying over the aerodrome! Sure enough, at some 5,000 feet in the sky above Maubeuge trespassed a Taube, with its unmistakable scalloped wing. Within minutes Louis Strange was airborne in his Henry Farman, with Lieutenant Penn Gaskell in the observer's seat in front of him, armed with the Lewis gun that Louis had brought across the Channel. They had mounted the weapon purely on their own initiative. Other fliers and some armament manufacturers had

31

experimented with gun mountings on the ground, and some had actually flown with a machine-gun before hostilities. But Louis Strange was the first British pilot to take a machine-gun into the air with the express intention of shooting an enemy aircraft out of it. Unfortunately, not even his airmanship could coax the overloaded Farman to 5,000 feet. 'An aerial joke, like the Daddy Long Legs', Cecil Lewis would call the Farman. [3] It certainly wasn't built for war. With a touch of disdain perhaps, the unmolested Taube turned and flew slowly back whence it had come.

When he landed, a frustrated Louis Strange was ordered to abandon the Lewis gun. If he must go hunting, he was told, he should arm his observer with a rifle. But he and Penn Gaskell had shown the way. Nor were they finished with their machine-gun.

The excitement occasioned by this first attempt at aerial combat was tempered later that day when it was reported that Lieutenants Waterfall and Bayly had been shot down by rifle fire from German infantry near Enghien and had died in the wreckage of their Avro.

Within two days, the troops of the BEF, who had marched so proudly towards the Front, were streaming back past the airfield. Their bands were no longer playing. Instead they were accompanied by the crump of German shellfire. The retreat from Mons had begun. The British had fought well against vastly superior numbers, but, in danger of being outflanked, had been forced to retire.

The RFC Squadrons were hastily withdrawn to Le Câteau. On his first reconnaissance flight from there, Louis Strange was shocked to see grey-green uniforms swarming where he had expected British khaki. When he hurried back to Le Câteau to report his observations, the aerodrome had been abandoned. He flew south, found the red Bovril lorry amongst the slow shuffle of traffic, landed alongside it and was told that the Squadrons were regrouping on a recently cut cornfield near St-Quentin. After another day of reconnaissance in deteriorating weather, shellfire drove them from their cornfield to fly at 300 feet in heavy rain to other unprepared fields around La Fère. Then it was retreat again, to Senlis, then Juilly, where, with a contingent of the Irish Light Horse, Louis Strange and his colleagues kept guard throughout the night against a force of Uhlans reported to be gathering in nearby woods. Then back to Senlis, then Melun. Always backwards, amidst the confusion and rumour of an army in retreat; sleeping in their 'valises' under the wings of their aircraft; eating when and what they could; and flying whenever the poor weather allowed, in an attempt to read some order into the military chaos below their fragile wings.

'Heavy fighting just north of Le Câteau', wrote Louis Strange in his log-book after three sorties on 24th August.

'Pace of retreat terrific. Saw isolated groups still holding out north of Guise', on the 26th.

'Transport, infantry, cavalry, guns all mixed up on roads south of Guise', on the 27th.

'Compiègne, Senlis burning a good deal. Germans still coming on', on 2nd September.

Then, after sorties on the 3rd and 4th he wrote, 'Very good recce'. [4]

That was an understatement. He and his observer, Lieutenant Rabagliati, had been amongst the Allied fliers who saw the columns of the German First Army no longer in pursuit to the south, but swinging south-east. It was a sighting that was to prove vital to the outcome of the battle. Unwittingly, the German commander, Von Kluck, was putting his head into an Anglo-French noose and exposing his right flank to counter-attack. Nobody knew of it amongst the still-retiring British and French armies. Reluctant at first to believe the reports from their airmen, Allied commanders eventually halted their retreat towards Paris, and struck back.

By 7th September, Louis Strange was writing after his day's flying above the Battle of the Marne, 'Going forward. Everyone in great hopes.' [4]

The tide had turned. Sir John French, commanding the BEF, was quick to acknowledge in a formal letter to the War Office that the turning of that grey tide was due largely to the intelligence provided by the eyes of the RFC.

As the Germans were driven back to the River Aisne, and after abortive attempts both by German and British armies to outflank each other along the Channel coast, the mobile warfare of Mons and the Marne ground to a halt. From the Channel to the Alps the combatant armies faced each other from behind rapidly fortified positions. The era of trench warfare on the Western Front had begun. Few foresaw how long it would last, nor the terrible toll it would take – on the ground and in the air.

Aerial reconnaissance had proved its value, and remained the primary purpose of the military aeroplane. Other roles, however, were being explored, mainly through the individual initiatives of the fliers themselves. And few showed more initiative during those first months of aerial warfare than Louis Strange . . .

Just as he had been the first to attempt to engage the enemy in the air with a machine-gun, so he was amongst the earliest to inflict damage on the enemy below. Keen to put into effect the bombing skills that he had learned from Claude Grahame-White during his ragtime flying days at Hendon, he had spent the morning of 28th August making three petrol bombs and attaching them to his Henry Farman:

> in the afternoon Penn Gaskell and I went to try them out. We dropped
> two bombs on either side of the road north of St-Quentin, where we
> found a lot of German transport; returning ten minutes later to have
> another go at the same lot, we found them moving south, so we dropped
> down to a low height and flew along over the road, where we managed to
> plant our third bomb right onto a lorry, which took fire and ran into a
> ditch. The lorry behind it caught fire as well, and both were well ablaze
> when we left. It was not a serious loss to the German army, but it sent us
> home very well pleased with ourselves.[1]

Other pilots tried similar tactics with grenades. Soon, 10-lb bombs were being issued. Then there were the canisters of pencil-size steel darts known as *fléchettes* to be tipped over the heads of German troops. They proved highly ineffective, but came in handy for a game of darts in the Mess. On such a scale did the bombing war begin.

As opposing lines of static defence were established along the Western Front, it became important that military commanders should be aware of the strength and position of enemy lines, and of any significant movement of troops behind them that might presage an assault. Aerial reconnaissance, now enhanced by aerial photography, would provide the answers. Artillery 'spotting', as conducted by Louis Strange with his gunnery observer, Lieutenant Furze, during much of late September and throughout October, was likely to assume greater significance as the technicalities of communication were improved.

But were these aerial spies to be allowed to go about their business unmolested? Certainly not! They must be shot out of the sky, decided the army commanders on both sides. And since anti-aircraft fire from the ground was unlikely by itself to achieve this, other aircraft must do the job. Thus the concept of an armed 'fighter' for this purpose began to take shape. However, the concept was in advance of technology. Whilst senior commanders stated the requirement and whilst aeroplane manufacturers of the warring nations addressed the problems of producing an aircraft light enough, yet sufficiently powerful to carry offensive armament and deny the sky to others, the fliers at the front continued to use their initiative.

Louis Strange had been forced to lay aside his machine-gun, but not his offensive zeal. He changed the controls of his Henry Farman from the back seat to the forward nacelle and equipped his now rear-mounted observer with a safety-belt – itself a novelty – that would enable him to stand up and fire his rifle in any direction. He was not alone in such aggressive initiatives. His colleague, Norman Spratt, had the idea of tying a hand-grenade to a length of cable and trying to dangle it into the whirling propeller of an enemy plane. He was with difficulty dissuaded from attempting it. Aerial encounters remained few. When they did occur, the exchange of rifle and revolver fire was mostly ineffective, although several German planes were forced down by a combination of threatening shots and 'offensive' flying – one by Norman Spratt, without his suspended grenade.

Offensive prospects looked up when in early October No. 5 Squadron received a single-seat Bristol Bullet, so named because of its supposed speed of 100 mph. It was unarmed, until the Squadron's combined ingenuity equipped it with a rifle with a sawn-off stock, clamped to the side of the fuselage to shoot diagonally forward, thus missing the propeller. Major Higgins as Squadron Commander claimed the vehicle for himself. Which was a pity. His notoriously poor eyesight compounded the problems of first of all finding an enemy aeroplane, then aiming the off-set weapon. He buzzed through the skies in his Bullet with great zest but little effect.

Then to No. 5 came an Avro-504 with an 80-hp Gnome rotary engine driving a tractor propeller. It became Louis Strange's new mount. It is a tribute to his airmanship that of the planes that had left Gosport two months earlier, by mid-October his Henry Farman No. 341 was the only one still being flown by the Squadron. He patted it goodbye, then welcomed the new Avro. It offered him what he had been waiting for: the capability to take that Lewis gun back into the air. With the equally enthusiastic Penn Gaskell, he installed a cross-bar between the central struts, over which a rope was slung to haul the weapon into a position from which the front-seated o' server could fire it backwards over the head of the pilot. Forward fire would have removed the propeller.

On 22nd November, returning from reconnaissance near Lille with Lieutenant Small as his observer instead of Penn Gaskell, Louis Strange encountered an Aviatik, a German two-seater, 7,000 feet above Armentières. He gave chase:

> I turned in front of the Aviatik and about 200 feet above it, signalling to Small to hold his fire until I was ready.
> I turned half left, kept my eye on the Aviatik, and dived across his front just as hard as I could drive my old Avro. When I was in position I nodded to Small, who replied with a good long burst from the Lewis gun . . . By keeping my eyes fixed on the Aviatik's left top aileron, I managed

to maintain my position and correct distance. After a second burst I came up closer, being then about fifty feet below the enemy, but the German pilot must have gone into a slight turn without banking, for I suddenly saw his observer lean out and fire a clip of cartridges from his Loeber pistol. Then the Aviatik slipped across, and a few moments later that observer was potting at me from the other side.

Small was changing a drum at the time. I saw a look of surprise and pain come over his face and then noticed that his glove was covered with blood. All the same Freddy Small worked hard at his drum, and was ready to open fire again as soon as I had manoeuvred the Avro into position. He had shot away about half another drum when suddenly the Aviatik pulled up, stalled, and side-slipped away at a vertical angle.

I was desperately afraid that he was going to escape me, but I dived ahead, and both machines went down at a terrific speed . . . I had to hustle ahead of him to cut him off from his own lines.

I just managed to head him off, but he doubled back to the left . . . We were down to 500 feet at this time, but only a mile from the front line; I dived ahead again, but the Aviatik flattened out to land, and I cursed fiercely when I thought that I had lost him. A stream of black exhaust came from his Mercedes engine, and it looked as though he was just going to streak over the trenches a few feet above the ground, but with a last effort I shot in front of him again.

Down went the Aviatik's nose; it flattened out over a hedge and made a bumpy landing in a ploughed field just behind a wood where the Cornwalls and Devons occupied some reserve trenches. I knew they would do their share of the business, and as it was too close to the firing-line for me to land and I had a wounded observer to get home, I headed full speed for Bailleul.[1]

Louis Strange had claimed his first enemy aircraft.

The downing of one aircraft by another was still a rare occurrence. Ground-fire was at that time a greater hazard than aerial combat. Long-range anti-aircraft fire – 'Archie' in popular parlance – was innacurate, but the sheer volume of exploding metal flung into the sky was bound to claim victims. Even more dangerous was the rifle and machine-gun fire directed at aircraft flying at lower altitudes. It persuaded some pilots to fly with a flattened steel helmet under their backsides. Louis Strange recalled an instance when cloud forced him to carry out his reconnaissance at 3,500 feet. For forty-five minutes he provided a slow-flying target for an unusually heavy concentration of German gunners: 'At one time shells were simply all around us; in addition to the deafening roar of their bursts we could easily hear the whistle and shriek of bullets, which was all very awe-inspiring.' [1]

It was a game of chance, played every day, though not always against such odds.

Nor were all the bullet and shrapnel holes which Allied aeroplanes carried back to their fields caused by Germans. To most troops in the trenches one flying-machine was much like another, and since aeroplanes had acquired this habit of dropping beastly things, it was healthier to shoot first and find out who they belonged to afterwards. Louis's good friend Gordon Bell was amongst the first to be downed by French rifles. With a holed engine and an injured knee he crash-landed in a tree and was flung clear. When a staff officer galloped up and called, 'I say, have you crashed?' Gordon, a stutterer when annoyed, replied, 'No . . . I always b . . . b . . . b . . . bloody land like that!' [5]

The introduction of red, white and blue roundels as a more obvious identification than the Union Jack originally painted on British aircraft lessened but did not eliminate the hazard of 'friendly' fire. 'Believed by none and fired at by all,' would long remain the ironic cry of the 'recce' pilots.

An even greater threat to those pioneer fighting machines than shell or bullet was the fragility of their own frames and the uncertainty of their engines. During 1914 more aeroplanes and crews were lost through flying accident than by enemy action. Flimsy, underpowered machines, not built for the strains of aerial combat, were flown from rough fields and maintained in conditions of almost constant dampness that caused fabric to sag, wooden spars to warp, engines to cough themselves into rattling wreckage.

The weather could be a fearsome enemy, both on the ground and in the air. The violent gales of the night of 12th September that caught the RFC unawares at Fère-en-Tardenois had strewn the field with heaps of splintered wood and tattered canvas. Only a dozen aircraft had been able to take to the air the following morning. One of them had been Louis Strange's Henry Farman, old faithful No. 341. With a kingpost almost shot away by ground-fire during a reconnaissance flight, he had been forced to land and park the aircraft in the lee of a straw rick, in which he also took residence for the night. Wakened by the storm, he had used his countryman's skills to plait ropes of straw with which he piqueted the aeroplane to the ground. At dawn, with a new kingpost fitted, he had flown to join the other survivors of the tempest, and to reconnoitre the battlefield of the Aisne.

The prevailing wind was from the west. Throughout the war on the Western Front, as the RFC pursued its policy of taking the aerial conflict to the enemy, those westerlies would claim many allied fliers whose inexperience or over-confidence took them too far and kept them too long down-wind of their own lines. If those winds brought the additional hazard of low cloud, there were no flying instruments to give a pilot his balance when his horizons disappeared. Such circumstances tested even Louis Strange's airmanship. After a dawn reconnaissance south of Lille in November, he found himself with his observer, Arkwright, in strengthening westerly winds and cut off from 'home' by a rapidly advancing storm:

The snow line was now sweeping up to the northern outskirts of Lille. 'The longer you look at it, the less you like it,' I said to myself, thinking of some of the big doubles in the Blackmoor Vale in my hunting days. I crammed my helmet down on my head, pushed the throttle wide open and headed straight into that nasty black cloud . . . in less time than it takes to write these words, I found myself surrounded by pitch blackness, in which the bumps were terrific.

It was hopeless trying to keep control of the machine; I was completely at the mercy of the storm centre into which I had headed. I just took advantage of every chance allowed me by the elements; when the wires screamed I throttled back, and when I encountered a momentary lull I pushed the stick forward. Sometimes I felt as though I was sitting on air, while all the weight of my body was thrown onto my belt; then I could think of nothing but how to roll the machine the right way up. When I side-slipped the fact was indicated to me by the howling draught on the side of my face.

I knew we were rapidly losing height, and therefore throttled down and waited for the ground to show up through the whirl of snow, although I did not know at what angle above or below me it would appear . . .

Suddenly it got quite light and I saw snowflakes all around me. Then a church spire, upside-down, hove into sight just up over my top left-hand wing-tip. My instinct told me to put it the right way up, and somehow I managed to do it. The church spire flicked out of sight and then appeared on my right in a more reasonable attitude.

I had just flattened the machine out when the wheels hit the ground lightly. Up we bounced as I opened the engines full out, and then I saw straight ahead of me a line of hangars, into which men were wheeling machines that I recognised as German by the black crosses on their wings. Our Avro sailed over the top of them, but not a sound of gunfire was heard except that which came from our own machine-gun. Whatever Arkwright's feelings were during the storm, they had not impaired his presence of mind.

I knew that we were probably over Fives Aerodrome at Lille, and so scraped over the housetops . . . I held on until I found the canal and then flew along it northward at about a hundred feet. It was a trying business, because Arkwright let fly at all sorts of targets with the Lewis gun, and the row nearly cracked my eardrums . . . We scraped over the trenches, to the accompaniment of a few stray shots, and landed at Bailleul in the falling snow . . . [1]

The weather, the enemy and the fragility of machines took their toll during that autumn and early winter. Apart from a brief leave in Dorset in early December, recorded in his log-book as 'three good days hunting', Louis Strange had flown continuously over the Western Front on reconnaissance, artillery spotting and 'opportunity' bombing missions. By the end of the year he was the only pilot left in B Flight of those who had crossed the Channel with the RFC less than five months before. His friends were recovering from injuries, or dead.

As a body, those who first flew into battle with the RFC were unique. The time had not yet come when men would choose to join or transfer to the Flying Corps as a less disagreeable alternative to trench warfare, or would be attracted to it by the glamour of wings on a distinctive uniform. This initial breed of combat pilots were volunteer fliers in the truest sense, lured into the air by lust for adventure, held there by a discovered love of flight. They had learned to fly at civilian schools at their own expense, which placed them amongst the socially favoured. They were gentleman adventurers – visionaries too in their perception of the aeroplane as a weapon of war. To fly at all in 1914 required unusual boldness and a touch of eccentricity amounting almost to lunacy. Flight implied rebellion against the accepted order of things, which in a military environment manifested itself in disdain for regulations and conventions. The youthful RFC had no traditions to guide its young men; the young men were about to create those traditions themselves.

They were men of immense spirit, great originality and fine disregard for military pomp and authority.

Men like Robert Smith Barry, who later, as Squadron Commander, would burn his office down to rid himself of untended paperwork, and of whom Trenchard would say, with considerable understatement, 'though a genius among pilots he was an eccentric among administrators'.

Men like Gordon Shepherd, who as Commanding Officer of No. 6 Squadron when it paraded in pouring rain for King George in 1915 would write, 'I wonder if HM realises what a severe strain to loyalty these visits are. If not, his staff should tell him.'

Men like Louis Arbon Strange, who on Christmas Day in 1914,

when the rest of 5 Squadron were enjoying the contents of the RFC Air Committee gift-hampers and the gilt boxes of chocolates sent by Princess Mary for every officer and man, took off alone in his Avro, flew across the stilled lines, and dropped a football on Lille airfield to go bouncing amongst the startled Germans.

CHAPTER FOUR

Flight Commander on the Western Front

The year 1915 began well for Louis Strange. He was sent to Vincennes for two weeks to test-fly the new French Voisin. He didn't think much of the aeroplane, but enjoyed Paris. His visit was enlivened by the company of his ragtime flying friend and former mentor from Hendon, Louis Noel, now flying for the French Aviation Militaire. Even so, he was not sorry to get back to Bailleul.

An increasing number of his flights over the Front now involved the new science of photographic reconnaissance, with the primary purpose of mapping enemy trench lines. It was a role that offered little opportunity for hunting Huns with a Lewis gun. Instead the Avro became the hunted, for the necessity to fly straight and level above enemy heads while the observer man-handled the bulky camera attracted much hostility from Archie. One of Louis Strange's last sorties with 5 Squadron almost became his last flight ever:

> Our familiarity with the German gunners was of the type that breeds contempt, but at last they landed us with what must have been very nearly a direct hit. At any rate, a great piece of metal came up through the floor of our machine, passing through the petrol-tank that formed the front seat and taking its departure through the top plane. It was a miracle that neither of us was hit, for the beastly thing carried away a bit of my boot and a bit of Gladstone's coat, in addition to drenching us with petrol from the punctured tank. [1]

Hazards were not confined to the air, as Captain Carmichael recalled in his recollections of 5 Squadron:

> In mid-February another case of sabotage was suspected when the Squadron's store of Verey lights, ammunition and grenades went skyward, and Strange who was Duty Officer that night imperturbably enjoyed another of his many adventures before leaving on promotion as Flight Commander to No. 6 Squadron. [2]

Louis Strange was surprised to be promoted to Captain, delighted to be given command of a Flight, but sorry to leave 5 Squadron. He was

41

particularly sorry to leave his Avro, for 6 Squadron flew the BE-2c, which was not a machine on which he could mount a Lewis gun.

He didn't have far to move: his new Squadron quarters were just across the Bailleul airfield behind the old lunatic asylum. But within a few days No. 6, under Major Gordon Shepherd, moved to Poperinghe to support the battle about to break over Neuve Chappelle. 'No hangars, no billets, beastly wet day', complained Louis Strange to his log-book on arrival at the new field. [3]

On his second sortie from Poperinghe, Louis Strange won the Military Cross. Had he not survived the flight, it is likely that he would have become the first flier to be awarded the Victoria Cross, for it was a time when martyrs were more honoured than survivors.

He and several others left their observers behind that day, and loaded their aircraft with bombs instead. Their targets were railway stations behind the German lines, their orders to disrupt enemy communications as the battle for Neuve Chapelle was unleashed. It was the first time that aircraft had been despatched on a bombing raid as an integral part of a battle plan. Previous bombing had been on an opportunity basis and as a secondary feature of reconnaissance flights. This was the beginning of tactical bombing as a defined task. Louis Strange's log-book, unusually informative on this occasion, tells the story:

> Got a good show at last. Sent to drop three 35-lb bombs on Courtrai
> station. Crossed lines at 5,000 feet at Hollebeke. Got hit by AA gun. V.
> cloudy and misty, nearly got lost. Saw River Lys and Courtrai well to the
> south, kept straight on and turned to the east of Courtrai and when about
> three miles behind some clouds, dived through them down to about 500
> feet but came out about one mile short of the station. Kept nose down
> and flew just over top of railway right into the station. Saw a sentry at
> end of platform who fired as I came towards him. I threw a hand-grenade
> just as I got to him. Rifle fire from all directions. Released bombs from
> 50 feet right in the station on two trains standing with steam up on the
> main lines. All must have gone off as the noise was terrific, pulled
> machine up and looking over my shoulder saw a big column of smoke.
> Just missed some high telegraph wires. Made for the open country south
> of Courtrai, got fired on from each village, returned south of the Lys and
> had difficulty with clouds. Arrived back at about 5 p.m. It was great
> sport . . . [3]

It was later reported that the trains had been crowded with German troops, of whom some 75 were killed or injured. More importantly, rail traffic through the station was blocked for three days. For this and 'other acts of gallantry' Captain Louis Strange was awarded the Military Cross. When Lieutenant Rhodes Moorhouse carried out a similar but less effective raid on Courtrai in April, he was less fortunate. Wounded by ground-fire, he managed to return his machine to Merville and make his report before collapsing. He died the following day. His bravery brought the RFC its first Victoria Cross.

On 22nd April, Louis Strange experienced another 'first'. With Lieutenant Hawkins as observer, he was cruising above the Ypres salient at 5,000 feet, watching for gun flashes in the fading light to mark the positions of German artillery. He suddenly noticed streams of yellowish-green smoke coming from the German lines. Puzzled, he dropped to 2,000 feet. The evil-coloured clouds were drifting slowly down on the trenches occupied by French colonial troops. He suddenly recalled the generally discounted rumour that the Germans were preparing to use poison gas. He swung the nose of the BE-2c to the west and rammed the throttle open. At Poperinghe he and Hawkins jumped into a tender and were bounced to 5th Army Headquarters to report personally to General Plummer. They had witnessed the first gas attack of the war, one that opened the battle called Second Ypres that tore a 4-mile gap in the Allied lines which could have resulted in a major breakthrough had the Germans followed up with more confidence.

The battle of Neuve Chapelle had been the first major attempt by British forces in 1915 to break through the German defensive line. Attempts at a massive outflanking movement through the Dardanelles had foundered disastrously at Gallipoli and, as the only apparent alternative to outflanking, a series of costly frontal assaults on the great trench barrier that stretched across Europe had been set in train. At Neuve Chapelle, after initial success the British impetus foundered through sheer hesitancy, poor communications and shortage of artillery shells. After plugging the hole in the Ypres salient created by the gas attack, the Allies tried again.

One of the problems faced by Commanders at Neuve Chapelle had been a lack of information about the positions of their advancing troops. To overcome this, when a further offensive was launched against Aubers Ridge in May a system of 'contact patrols' by the RFC was established, whereby troops would mark their advanced positions with ground panels, to be noted and reported by aircrews. The system failed at Aubers, partly because of poor visibility, but primarily because there was no advance. The Germans were better prepared than at Neuve Chapelle. British troops walked into a wall of machine-gun fire. The assault was pressed for two days, after which the British had no shells left and few men.

Those flying above the slaughter, desperately trying to pierce the fog of battle, were not unaware of the horrors of ground combat. Forced landings near the line were not uncommon, and there were occasional liaison visits to forward trenches, from which they came away grateful for the comparative freedom of the skies. On one such visit to the First Battalion of the Dorsetshire Regiment, Louis was delighted to meet a familiar figure. Fudge Maidment had been a Spetisbury poacher before enlisting, and had taught the youthful Louis how to decoy ducks out of the Stour, set night lines for pike and lay snares for rabbits. His main complaint to 'Captain' Louis was about the food in the trenches.

Louis Strange's inbred love of the land never left him. He accepted the horrors and dangers of war as the expected lot of the fighting man, but when they reached out to claim the innocents of the soil, he was outraged. Next to the airfield at Poperinghe an old farmer who refused to let the war disrupt the seasonal tending of the land had for several days been ploughing, with a mule and an ox. Louis wrote:

> I listened to him calling to the animals, and it struck me that the sounds proceeding from his mouth were very much the same as those used by our Dorsetshire ploughmen when they address their horses. But his field was never finished, because a stray bomb from a German machine on its way to have a shot at our aerodrome fell right on the plough, killing both the farmer and his two animals.' [1]

The incident appeared to shock him more than the great military tragedies of the war.

Although Louis Strange was not able to mount a machine-gun on his BE-2c, German planes seemed to be carrying increasingly heavy weaponry into the air. During an artillery observation sortie over the Ypres salient he came under machine-gun fire from a belligerent but innacurate Aviatik. After its sixth attack, Louis Strange's patience ran out. He ceased his evasive action and took the offensive, pouncing on the Hun out of a setting sun. One close-range shot from Lieutenant Awcock's rifle was enough. It must have caught the pilot, for the Aviatik rolled into a vertical spin and disappeared into the haze of battle over Houthulst Forest.

Death was never far away. Bullets and shrapnel were constant companions in the sky. On one occasion, under machine-gun attack by two German aircraft whilst well over enemy lines, one cylinder of Louis Strange's Renault engine cut out. He managed to evade the attackers, then:

We struggled painfully back until we reached Menin where we were literally smothered in shellfire from the Archies. The black and white bursts around us looked a solid mass, and the din was terrific, but we could do nothing but plod steadily onwards as we were now down to 2,000 feet and still losing height. Holes began to appear in the fabric of our wings, while the oil-pressure gauge went down to nil and the engine started vibrating badly. Then I suddenly saw a tear appear on the shoulder of De Halpert's flying jacket and thought he must have been wounded.

Our next bit of trouble occurred when a lump of shrapnel smashed the rev counter in my cockpit, but I ought to have looked on it as a blessing in disguise, because it mercifully put me out of the agony of watching the engine revs gradually drop back. But all bad times come to some sort of an end, and so we scraped over the trenches at about 800 feet, and were thankful to land behind a small wood just out of range of any serious shelling. To my relief I found that De Halpert was unwounded, a splinter of shell having torn his coat without grazing his skin; but we were both annoyed to have had such a rotten trip . . . [1]

On another occasion a splinter of metal tore a hole in his leg. When he returned to Poperinghe he doused it with iodine and bandaged it himself to avoid being sent to base hospital and a probable grounding. He explained away his limp as sciatica, which was unfortunately prophetic.

Throughout the inconclusive land battles of that spring and summer, and during the sporadic trench warfare between them, artillery observation, increasingly with wireless communication, and reconnaissance with eye and camera remained the primary task of the hard-pressed fliers. But as each side sought to deny the other the freedom of airborne observation, aerial combat became increasingly common. The need for fighter aircraft was first recognised by equipping squadrons with one or more planes better suited for aerial nastiness. In May, No. 6 Squadron received two single-seat Martinsyde 'scouts'. The Martinsyde was an unstable machine, hardly superior in speed and rate of climb to the Avro and BE-2c, but in the eyes of Louis Strange these defects were outweighed by the Lewis gun mounted on its upper wing. He and fellow Flight Commander Lanoe Hawker laid first claim to these early fighters, but Louis Strange's relationship with the Martinsyde was not to be a happy one . . .

His first flight in it almost ended in disaster. High over Ypres, climbing after an Albatross two-seater, a lucky long-range shot from the German observer ruptured the Martinsyde's oil-tank. Castor oil flooded the floor of the aircraft. As the liquid slopped towards the rear, the machine became tail-heavy and slid into a tail-stall and spin. As Louis recovered the aircraft, the weight of oil slurped forwards, taking the nose down. The only way out of that was to push the Martinsyde onto its back and roll it out. Then the oil-starved engine seized and stopped. Unable to put the nose down into a glide, the luckless pilot managed to side-slip the aircraft through the final 3,000 feet to a heavy landing on a narrow track between fields of hop-poles. It was a ragtime flying performance that would have drawn roars of approval from the spectators at pre-war Hendon.

His next escape was even more dramatic, and would take its place amongst the annals of outstanding aerial misadventures.

Trading shots with an Aviatik at some 8,000 feet above Menin, Louis emptied the drum of his Lewis gun. When he tried to change it he found the used drum had jammed. Probably a twisted thread. He wedged the stick between his knees and, standing up in the cockpit, tugged at the obstinate drum with both hands, spurred by the whistle and whip of bullets from the Aviatik. Inadvertently, his knees loosened their grip on the stick. The Martinsyde, already climbing at its maximum angle, stalled and flicked over into a spin, hurling its pilot from the cockpit. Louis Strange found himself hanging in the air beneath his inverted machine, clinging with both hands to the drum of the Lewis gun. Only a few seconds previously he had been cursing the twisted thread; if it came loose now, he was dead. The luxury of a parachute had not yet been accorded to fliers. Needing to improve that slender hold on life, he let go the drum with one hand and made a grab in the general direction of the central section strut. He found it, and transferred his other hand:

My chin was rammed against the top plane, beside the gun, while my legs were waving about in empty air. The Martinsyde was upside-down in a flat spin, and from my precarious position the only thing I could see was the propeller (which seemed unpleasantly close to my face), the town of Menin, and the adjacent countryside. Menin and its environs were revolving at an impossible angle and getting larger with every turn. I began to wonder what sort of spot I was going to crash on. Then I got angry and cursed myself for wasting time on such idle speculations, while it dawned on me that my only chance of righting the machine lay in getting my feet in the cockpit . . . I kept on kicking upwards behind me until at last I got one foot and then the other hooked inside the cockpit. Somehow I got the stick between my legs again, and jammed on full aileron and elevator; I do not know exactly what happened then, but the trick was done. The machine came over the right way up, and I fell off the top plane into my seat with a bump . . . [1]

Louis Strange's celebrated tussle with his Martinsyde scout in 1915 would – a generation later – be reconstructed by the popular magazine, *Top Spot* (*The Amalgamated Press Ltd*)

His troubles were not over. That 'bump' had smashed the seat and jammed the controls. He managed to hurl the wreckage of the seat clear and so free the cables, just in time to pull the Martinsyde out of its headlong dive and clear the trees alongside the Menin road by a matter of feet. The pilot of the Aviatik later recorded that, having seen the British pilot flung from his cockpit, he had been so assured of a kill that he had not bothered to follow the aircraft down.

The American 'ace' Ira Jones, in relating this episode in his own memoirs, provided a fitting postscript: 'Strange flew back to his aerodrome, and I was told that he slept for about thirteen hours without waking. A man without his presence of mind, courage, and resource would be sleeping still.' [4]

Most flights by Louis Strange and Lanoe Hawker in the Martinsyde were frustrated by the aircraft's inability to close with the higher-flying German aircraft which, once they caught sight of the mounted machine-gun, usually lifted away to safer altitudes. A more suitable aircraft for the combat role was the Bristol Scout. Louis Strange had returned briefly to England early in May to collect one of these neat little single-seaters from Farnborough and deliver it to Abeele, but No. 6 Squadron didn't receive its first until July. As senior Flight Commander, Lanoe Hawker claimed the new Bristol. Louis Strange helped him mount a Lewis gun on the left side of the fuselage, fixed to shoot forwards and outwards at an angle that would avoid the propeller arc. This would require any attack to be suitably crab-like.

Hawker scored two unconfirmed victories early in July, then on the 15th he in the Bristol and Louis Strange in the Martinsyde took off as a pair. They had planned that the Martinsyde, as the less effective fighter, would act as decoy for the Bristol. The trap worked. An unsuspecting Aviatik, nosing after the apparently unconcerned Martinsyde, was pounced upon by Hawker and sent crashing to earth between the British forward and reserve trenches on the Menin Front. On a second sortie that day Hawker shot down a Rumpler. At that time and in such a machine, to shoot down two aircraft in one day was an extraordinary feat, and brought Lanoe Hawker the first Victoria Cross to be awarded for aerial combat. He was the prototype of the fighter ace of an era yet to come.

But in 1915 neither Lanoe Hawker, Louis Strange nor any other fliers were fighter pilots. First and foremost they remained reconnaissance pilots, operating in direct support of the Army formations to which each squadron was attached. Only when those primary tasks had been carried out could pilots climb into the Martinsyde or the Bristol scout and go hunting for the Hun in the sky. During that hard-pressed summer such opportunities for offensive patrols were rare. And when they did find their Hun and when they did manage to send him diving or spinning away, rarely did they follow him down to confirm a kill. The altitude they had so laboriously gained was more precious than keeping the score. Thus the terse 'Downed another Hun' in the log-books of Louis Strange and other offensive pilots of that era was not always reflected in official records.

Also to the RFC and to No. 6 Squadron that summer came the FE-2a, a two-seater pusher which, as well as providing a much improved vehicle for reconnaissance and artillery spotting, was capable of offensive and defensive fire from a forward-mounted machine-gun. Still not fast enough, Louis Strange told his log-book, but definitely an improvement over the BE-2c and the Avro.

He didn't stay long enough in France to enjoy the improvement.

One evening in early August he was called into the Squadron Commander's office. 'A brilliant leader' would be Louis Strange's subsequent recollection of Gordon Shepherd, who would die in the air in the later stages of the war. His refreshing disrespect for pompous authority appealed to Louis. 'Kitchener and Asquith came round the other day,' Gordon Shepherd wrote on 10th July. 'I was told they were coming and might have made preparations if I had thought the present War Ministry worthy of such.' [5]

But on that August evening in 1915, Louis Strange had a vigorous disagreement with his Commanding Officer. Gordon Shepherd handed him a list of names. They were the original thirty-seven pilots who had flown out to France a year before.

'How many of these chaps are still out here, Louis?' he asked.

Louis Strange didn't need to look at the list. He already knew. For two months he had been the longest-serving flier on the Western Front. He sensed what was coming, but had to admit that he was the only one left of the 'originals'.

'That settles it then,' said Gordon Shepherd. 'I'm posting you to Home Establishment. Tomorrow.'

Louis argued forcefully but to no avail. Gordon Shepherd was a wise man, perhaps ahead of his time in anticipating the accumulative effects on a combat flier of constant exposure to harsh elements, mechanical uncertainty, bullet and shell. Almost daily for twelve months Louis Strange had flown with death never far away, sometimes breathing on him all too closely. No man could fail to be affected by such exposure. He would not have admitted to it, even had he realised it. Good airmanship and good luck had kept him alive during his first year of war in the air. His attitude towards it seems to have changed little during that time. He had fought with courage and an *élan* not uncommon amongst his fellows, sprinkling his log-book with much 'good hunting', 'good show', 'great sport'. He evinced no hatred of Germans. He fought them because it was what his country expected of him. He was of a patriotic breed in a patriotic age. But if his spirit was undiminished by a year of combat flying, it is impossible to believe that he was physically unaffected. One need only look at photographs of later aces, of Boelcke and Guynemer and Lanoe Hawker himself – not the studio portraits posed for an admiring public, but the informal snapshots taken not long before death caught up with them. See the hollowed cheeks and the eyes staring at something out beyond the camera. Faces of men too long exposed to altitude sickness, to castor-oil fumes, to the mind-numbing vibrations and roar of flight, to sleepless nights, to death. Perhaps Gordon Shepherd saw the early signs of combat fatigue in Louis Strange's face after an unrivalled period of operational flight. He insisted that it was time for his Flight Commander and friend to take a break.

'Received orders to proceed to England. Feel very sick about it. Was having such a good time,' Louis Strange grumbled to his log-book on 2nd August 1915. [3]

Whilst passing through St-Omer on his reluctant return to England, Louis Strange looked in at the RFC Headquarters in France, where General Trenchard confirmed that he didn't want to see Strange back in France until he had taken a long rest and had risen to the command of a Squadron of his own. It didn't quite turn out that way . . .

After ten days' leave in Dorset, Louis learned that he was posted as Flight Commander to No. 12 Squadron, then forming at Nether-avon. He would be back on the Front within weeks! Jubilantly he hurried to join the Squadron, and with characteristic energy and initiative spent four hectic weeks training his crews and equipping his Flight's BE-2c aircraft with extra fuel-tanks, bomb-racks and wireless

The BE-2cs of No. 12 Squadron lined up for review at Netheravon before Louis Strange, as senior Flight Commander, led them to France in September 1915

sets. He also fitted bomb-sights and machine-gun mounts of his own devising. The latter would subsequently be adapted to most two-seater tractor-planes until superseded by the Scarf–Ring mounting. He found time occasionally to pop down to Spetisbury. 'Landed in Barn Field. Went home to tea,' records his log-book.

Major Newall, the Squadron Commander and later to become Chief of the Air Staff, crossed to France by sea in advance of the Squadron, and it was a proud Louis Strange who, after pausing at Folkestone and taking lunch at the Grand Hotel, led No. 12 Squadron across the Channel from Hawkinge – an airfield which he was to command in another, then unforeseen world war.

At St-Omer, the Squadron was inspected by General Trenchard. When he set eyes on Louis Strange, Trenchard asked what he was doing there, reminded him that he was supposed to be in England, told his Aide-de-camp (ADC) Maurice Baring to make a note of it – Maurice Baring was never without his notebook – and continued his inspection. Louis Strange hoped that the incident would be forgotten, or that his friend Maurice Baring would manage to mislay the note. He kept away from Headquarters and got on with the war. His first flight took him over the 'old hunting ground' and the German airfield at Lille. The days of dropping footballs were over. This time his calling card was a cluster of 25-lb bombs.

A few days later, No. 12 took delivery of a Bristol Scout. Because of his previous experience in the fighter, it was assigned to Louis Strange:

> much to my delight, as I imagined I was going to fly it instead of crawling about the air in a BE-2c. I was just fitting it up with a Lewis gun when General Trenchard came along, with Maurice Baring, his ADC.
> 'I thought I told you, Baring, to remind me to send Strange home?'
> he began; and then, turning to me, he boomed out, 'Go home at once, Strange.'
>   'Yes, sir,' I replied, saluting smartly.
>   'Go home at once, Strange,' he repeated, 'in that machine, now.'
>   His visit occurred about three in the afternoon. The wind was thirty-five miles per hour on the ground, while the machine to which he pointed was a dilapidated Maurice Farman. All the same I could do nothing but salute again and take him at his word; I therefore gave orders for the machine to be started up, and without bothering to look for helmet or goggles, got up in the nacelle and staggered off towards the west . . . [1]

Which was how a dispirited Louis Strange returned to Home Establishment in September 1915.

CHAPTER FIVE

Home Establishment . . . and to Hell with the Consequences

After a brief leave in Dorset, Louis Strange received his posting instructions. He was to proceed to Gosport, there to form and command No. 23 Squadron and have it at operational readiness by the 1st of January 1916.

He was overjoyed. To command one's own squadron was the ambition of every worthwhile flier. Although the daily task of a squadron was ordered by higher authority, the means of meeting that task and of administering the squadron were left to its commander, offering immense scope for flair and initiative. For Louis Strange, the posting also meant a swift return to the Western Front and an escape from what he saw as the suffocating clutches of Home Establishment. It looked as though Trenchard's wish for him to spend a tour of duty in England was to be circumvented yet again.

On 21st September Louis Strange flew into Gosport from Farnborough in Avro No. 4741. He was a high spirits, and rather proud of himself.

'I've come to command No. 23 Squadron,' he announced to the Station Commander.

'Never heard of it,' was the response.

'Ah . . . Then I suppose I'm it,' said Louis. It was to be one of those starting-from-scratch jobs at which he was to become so adept.

The following day he found himself an office, a telephone, a Sergeant and three men, an old 50-hp Gnome Blériot and the bits of two Henry Farmans. Within a week he had forty-four all-ranks under command, including several pilots who he immediately began to train in operational flying on the Avro that he had brought from Farnborough. That and the old Blériot were the Squadron's only aircraft, for its FE-2bs, he was told, would not be available until the end of the year. As soon as he considered them good enough, Louis assigned his four best pilots to instruction and personally badgered RFC Headquarters – 'sitting on doorsteps', he called it – into allocating three more Avros for training his crews. To make sure these aircraft were not snaffled by other predatory units, he sent three pilots to sit on the doorstep of A V Roe's Manchester factory with orders to collar the machines as soon as they emerged from the workshops and had done their first test-flight.

Louis Strange's emphasis on training sought not only to prepare pilots for combat but also to reduce the rate of aircraft accidents caused by poor airmanship, and so lessen the temporary or permanent loss of scarce machines. So successful was he in producing high-calibre pilots that RFC Headquarters began to poach his trained crews to replace losses at the Front or to assist in the formation of other squadrons. Because he went to the unusual length of training his pilots to fly at night, several were transferred to home defence against Zeppelins. He shrugged his shoulders and trained some more.

Amidst the constant round of training, administration, badgering and outright filching, he found time to get married to Marjorie, the girl he had taken for an adventurous flip at Hendon in 1913. The wedding was on 5th November in Saint Mark's, Audley Street. The best man was Major Lanoe Hawker VC, now commanding No. 24 Squadron, with which he would die a year later. Among the guests was Lieutenant General Sir David Henderson, who had commanded the RFC in France when Louis Strange and the other pioneer pilots had first gone to war in 1914. A welcome wedding gift was Louis's promotion to Major. There was no time for a honeymoon.

Louis Strange and his men were ready by the 1st of January as ordered, but still without their operational aircraft. Louis himself took delivery of the first FE-2b and flew it from Farnborough to Gosport on 18th January. Another eleven soon followed, and on 20th January, No. 23 was ordered to hold itself in readiness to proceed to France. To celebrate, the Squadron challenged its friendly rivals of No. 22, also forming at Gosport, to a rugby match. The result was uncertain, for nobody had kept the score, so after dinner play resumed on the aerodrome illuminated by car headlights.

Afterwards, Louis Strange felt much the worse for wear. But not because of the rugger, he discovered. The doctor diagnosed acute appendicitis. Louis was rushed to Cosham Military Hospital for immediate operation. It was apparently too much of a rush, for when they sewed him up, they left a swab inside his stomach. It was only discovered several days later, when continuing pain and his seriously deteriorating condition persuaded the doctors to open him up again. On a fine morning just before his second operation he experienced pain of a different sort as from his hospital window he watched the FE-2bs of No. 23 Squadron fly over the coastline on their way from Gosport to the Western Front.

It would be more than two years before he would follow them. Trenchard had got his way after all.

The two years that Louis Strange was to spend on Home Establishment would be put to wise and fruitful use by the RFC. Instead of the staff appointments that he would have loathed, he was to fill a succession of increasingly important training roles. To these posts he would bring, not only his talents as flier and instructor and his considerable front-line experience, but definite and sometimes radical training philosophies and methods. As he had demonstrated in his preparation of 23 Squadron, he was a believer in advanced training. He saw beyond the requirement for the straight-and-level flight of the reconnaissance pilot to the need for vigorous and instinctive manoeuvre, both to evade attack and to launch it, and realised too that the heavy rate of self-inflicted damage to machines and men within the RFC could be much reduced by improvements in basic airmanship. To carry out this training he saw a requirement for a cadre of professionally qualified instructors, within squadrons as well as at training units. They would need dual-control aircraft in which to impart their skills. Also, from the outset of his combat flying, Louis Strange had foreseen the decisive role that the machine-gun would play in aerial warfare, and was a firm advocate of gunnery training. In these views he was not alone, but amongst the minority. Most still looked upon the aeroplane as a dangerous beast, not to be given free rein. Stunt flying was still not encouraged in 1916, and forbidden altogether below 2,000 feet. It would take the even more radical activities of Louis's friend Robert Smith Barry to open the eyes of the RFC – indeed, of the whole aviation world, as Trenchard would later maintain – to more enlightened and purposeful flying training. But that was yet to come . . .

Louis Strange was almost four months in Cosham Hospital recovering from the mislaid swab. He was not the best of patients.

On his release from hospital he was posted to command the Machine Gun School at Hythe. Whether this was coincidence or whether someone at the Air Ministry actually remembered 1914 and thought, 'Ah, Louis Strange! The chap with the Lewis gun!' is not known. Probably the former, for the posting notice was annotated 'light duties'. Whoever wrote that couldn't have known Louis Strange. Twenty pupils each month were passing through the gunnery course when he went to Hythe; before he had completed six months of 'light duties' the monthly output had risen to 120.

The potential of the airborne machine-gun had advanced dramatically when the technical problems of firing forwards through the propeller arc of a tractor-plane had been overcome, first by the 'deflector plates' of Roland Garros (like Louis Strange, a pre-war stunt pilot), then more effectively by Anton Fokker's 'interruptor gear'. This was first used on the Fokker Eindekker with its single Parabellum machine-gun mounted on the cowling, and although the monoplane was itself a poor aircraft, the ability to point it directly at the enemy and pull the trigger gave the German pilots such an advantage in aerial combat that late 1915 became known as the era of the 'Fokker scourge'. This was countered in early 1916 by the appearance at the Front of the British DH-2. Once the difficulties of handling this quirky machine – it was known for a while as the 'Spinning Incinerator' – had been mastered, the single-seater pusher with its improved Lewis gun became more than a match for the Eindekker, particularly in the hands of Lanoe Hawker's aggressive 24 Squadron. Then came the French Nieuports and Spads, and the Sopwith 1½ Strutter, the first British aircraft to mount a forward-firing synchronised gun operated by the pilot, in addition to a Lewis for the rear-seated observer. From this was derived the single-seated Sopwith Pup which combined synchronised fire-power with delightful agility. By the time Louis Strange came to the Machine Gun School, aerial gunnery combined fixed weapons that fired along the trajectory of the aircraft with mobile weapons operated by the observer.

In both cases effective gunnery was seen as a combination of applied geometry and practice, plus guts enough to get lethally close to the enemy aircraft. Louis Strange could provide the geometry and a modicum of unopposed practice on the ground and in the air, but it was his belief that the most effective aerial killers were born, not made. The era of the aces – most of them lonely hunters – would

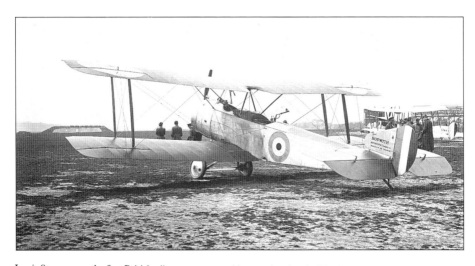

Louis Strange was the first British pilot to carry a machine-gun into battle. The Strange Gun Mounting – later adopted for a number of aircraft – is shown here on a Sopwith 1½ Strutter

suggest that he was right. His goal in 1916 was to raise the general standard of gunnery within the RFC, not to produce a handful of outstanding marksmen. Every pilot and observer should be able to shoot well; a few, by instinct, would be able to shoot better.

The actual training was the least of his problems. It was finding the equipment and the support facilities with which to furnish his rapidly expanding unit that exercised his initiative and determination, and which saw the flowering of his outstanding ability to get a job done against seemingly impossible administrative odds. His philosophy was devastatingly simple: the goal was everything, the means of achieving it of no consequence. Twenty-five years into the future, faced with similar logistical problems in his second world war, he would summarise his outlook thus: 'Do it!' he would say. 'If we wait for *proper channels* we'll never get the job done. Do it . . . And to hell with the consequences . . .' [1]

At Hythe in 1916 it was no good waiting for 'proper channels' to provide the wherewithal for the rapid expansion of the old Machine Gun School into No. 1 School of Aerial Gunnery. Louis Strange used the system of sitting-on-doorsteps at RFC Headquarters until someone gave him what he wanted, if only to get rid of him. This had already proved effective, if not always popular, in equipping No. 23 Squadron, and at Hythe he was ably supported by another arch scrounger in former Sergeant Major Chaney, who as a long-serving machine-gun instructor at Hythe had made the Lewis gun mounting for the Henry Farman that Louis Strange had flown to France in 1914. Now commissioned, Chaney was despatched to the Ministry on many doorstep-sitting forays. Between them, they milked what support they could from the War Office and RFC.

Louis Strange's measures to obtain local facilities were even more draconian. When September storms made his tented camp at Hythe no longer tenable, he requisitioned local boarding-houses in which to accommodate his trainees and staff, and when more pupils arrived he turned the guests out of the Imperial Hotel and requisitioned that too. He took over part of the Town Hall and other public buildings for lecture rooms. When his increased flying programme made it necessary to use the aerodrome at Lympne and the War Office refused to provide road transport, Louis took those of his staff and pupils who could drive a car to the Hythe depot of the Tilling and Stevens bus company and commandeered each bus as it came in from Folkestone. Then there was the golf course:

> There were headshakings when we took over the golf links for a rifle range. We were told that we simply could not do it, because Colonel

56

Somebody or other would have to do without his daily round of golf. I have no doubt the ancient warrior was patriotic enough to take the business in the right spirit, but I was too busy to find out. [2]

Most of these civilian assets were requisitioned without proper authority. If licensed civilians demanded to see a Ministry order, he would invent one, and announce in his firm but affable way that all claims for damage to business should be addressed to the War Office. He knew that he could be deep in trouble; but by the time the trouble came the job would be done.

After establishing No. 1 School of Air Gunnery at Hythe, Louis Strange was promoted to Lieutenant Colonel to form No. 2 School at Turnberry. Before taking that command, he thought that it was time to find out at first hand the current gunnery requirements of the fliers on the Western Front, so he spent four weeks in France. He went to the French School of Aerial Gunnery at Cazeaux, but found his visits to the British operational Squadrons more profitable. In particular he picked the brains of his friend Lanoe Hawker, whose No. 24 Squadron – the first to be equipped primarily as a fighter unit – had built a reputation amongst German as well as Allied airmen for aggressive flying in its DH-2s. In their conversations Hawker repeatedly stressed that the gun was only as good as the machine on which it was mounted. It was as though Lanoe Hawker foresaw his own fate, for Louis Strange would never see his friend again.

Although the DH-2 had been largely responsible for countering the Fokker scourge earlier in 1916, by autumn of that year it was obsolete. Outgunned, outpowered and often outnumbered by the sleek Albatrosses, as the opposing air forces fought bitterly for aerial supremacy above the bloody battles of the Somme, only Hawker's flying skill kept him alive. Until 23rd November . . .

On that day he fell in with a German pilot whose skill was no greater than his own but whose Albatross D-2 was vastly superior: Manfred von Richthofen. For almost half an hour they turned in their deadly circular dance, looking at each other across the space between their fiercely banked aircraft, the German using the power of his machine and Hawker relying on skill as each sought the other's tail. Over enemy territory and with fuel tanks almost empty, it was Hawker who had to break and run for home, dodging amongst treetops less than a hundred feet above the ground. But he could not escape the power of the Mercedes engine nor the bullets of the twin Spandau guns firing through the propeller arc of the Albatross. From a hundred feet Von Richthofen shot Louis Strange's 'best man' through the back of the head.

By then Louis Strange was at Turnberry, applying his late friend's firmly held belief that the outcome of the battle for the air depended upon capable gunnery, applied from suitable aircraft. Although the primary roles of the flying-machine remained reconnaissance, artillery observation and, to an increasing extent, direct support to the troops on the ground through bombing and strafing, an aeroplane could only carry out these functions under the protection of its own guns and those of escorting fighters. So Louis Strange preached and practised.

Providing moving targets in the air was a problem that he partly met by suspending small loads from parachutes. Inevitably he was accused of training pilots to slaughter the crews of German observation balloons when they tried to parachute to safety. Had he bothered to reply, Strange might have suggested that there was some merit in the idea.

Turnberry was a repetition of Hythe, a saga of scrounging, badgering and commandeering, but again Louis Strange was on the move before the repercussions of his unofficial but effective actions could bounce onto Air Ministry desks. He was sent to Loch Doon to set up a third gunnery school. He thought it an ideal location. In particular he was excited by the prospect of taking over the adjacent 9 miles of railway track on which to mount fast-moving targets. Before he could begin, political opinion and what he scoffed at as dismal lack of steadfast purpose caused the evacuation of this choice site. However, he was much cheered to learn that he was to return to more active flying.

In April 1917 he took up the post of Assistant Commandant of the Central Flying School at Upavon.

By 1917 ab-initio flying training had passed from CFS to a number of Reserve Squadrons, and experimental work had moved to Martlesham and Orfordness. CFS had become a centre of excellence for the advanced training of pilots, most of them destined to fly the new breed of 'scouts' – the Sopwith Camel and the SE-5. It was a prestigious post that Louis Strange now filled. Indeed, for several weeks between the departure of the Commanding Officer, Colonel MacLean, and the arrival of Colonel Jack Scott, he was in command of the School.

A centre of excellence it may have been, but in the spring of 1917 the call from the War Office was not for excellent pilots but for *any* pilots. Trenchard's policy of 'no empty seats' in the Messes of his front-line Squadrons meant that as fast as men were shot from the sky they must be replaced, albeit by fresh-faced youngsters with less than 15 hours of flying behind them instead of the 50 that was the CFS

As a Lieutenant Colonel, Louis Strange was Assistant Commandant of CFS at Upavon in 1917

target. Under such pressure, Louis Strange was much occupied with the administrative and logistic problems of squeezing as many flying hours as he could from limited resources.

He was also far from happy with the system and standard of instruction, which he considered to be overly cautious and a poor preparation for the demands of combat flying. He deplored in particular the absence of dual instruction in aircraft that did not readily forgive basic errors in airmanship.

Louis Strange was not alone in his opinion that flying training within the Service was woefully inadequate. Whilst he was doing what he could to improve matters at CFS, his former colleague from No. 5 Squadron, Robert Smith Barry, was similarly engaged at Gosport. the crash that had brought Smith Barry's service with 5 Squadron to a premature end in 1914 had shortened one leg by 2 inches and left him with a permanent limp that should have finished his career as a pilot. It didn't. Two years later he returned to the Front to fly with No. 60 Squadron, then to command it when its Commanding Officer, Major Waldron, was killed. 'A trifle eccentric, he was a fine pilot . . . his superiors sometimes found him a little trying . . .', the 60 Squadron history says of Smith Barry. An understatement, perhaps, for a man who set fire to much of his incoming mail and who addressed most of his own correspondence direct to Trenchard. That correspondence was much concerned with the inadequacies of his new pilots. He didn't just complain; he made detailed recommendations for changes to flying training. To his credit, Trenchard took Smith Barry at his word, and ordered him back to England to command No. 1 Reserve Squadron at Gosport. There Robert Smith Barry revolutionised flying training.

Instead of avoiding the problems of flight, such as stalling and spinning and cross-wind take-offs, he had his instructors and pupils deliberately seek them, thereby learning how to cope with difficulties before they had the added embarrassment of a Fokker on their tail. He didn't ban aerobatics; he *taught* them. His revolutionary methods succeeded largely because of emphasis on high instructional standards and dual control, using Avro-504s unofficially modified to his own specifications. He presented what became known as the 'Gosport System' in a training manual that by 1918 would be accepted as the bible of flying training.

Louis Strange had visited Smith Barry before taking up his appointment at Upavon. Their respect for each other was enormous. Much later in life Smith Barry would describe Louis Strange separately as 'the bravest man I ever knew' and 'the bravest man in the world', [3] while for his part Louis would credit his friend, as did most others, with the greatest contribution to flying training made by any one person. Undoubtedly the two benefited from an exchange of views and experiences early in 1917, but both were such individualists that their subsequent actions at their respective training establishments were independent rather than co-ordinated, and certainly not derivative. Two of a kind, they were. Fearless and outspoken innovators; rebels against unproductive tradition and red tape. Too much so for either of them ever to rise to high rank.

In June 1917 Louis Strange flew to France to study the latest developments in aerial fighting. For two weeks he toured the front-line airfields, and with No. 60 Squadron flew offensive patrols in a Nieuport Scout. He was impressed by the fighting spirit and skills of those pilots who had lived long enough to learn the harsh lessons of aerial combat, but was appalled – as were their squadron commanders – at the rawness of the new lads being sent out to 'fill the chairs' so rapidly emptied by the aerial battles being fought on the Arras Front.

He returned to Upavon even more convinced of the need for longer training, better training and above all for dual training in the new generation of aircraft. The first time a pupil flew one of the frisky scouts, he did so alone. The tremendous torque of the Camel's 130-hp Clerget rotary engine gave it a formidable right-hand turn that was valuable in combat but potentially lethal in the hands of a novice. Louis Strange had seen too many Camels come spinning out of the skies above Upavon; had listened to the terminal crunch of too much wood and fabric. Now, on his own initiative and with the help of his engineering officer, Lieutenant Morgan, he took the main fuel-tanks out of a number of Camels, replaced them with smaller ones, and used the additional space to fit the machines with dual controls. The accident rate fell, the training rate climbed. There was muttering at the Ministry about unauthorised modifications, but it was quickly muffled by the success of the dual training. Later, the SE-5 would also be converted, officially, to dual control, and Louis Strange would be the first to fly it at CFS.

He took it upon himself to test-fly most new machines as they appeared at Upavon – machines such as the new Bristol Scout, the Vickers Bullet and a Le Rhône-powered Bristol monoplane. He enjoyed such flying. But he would rather have been in France, fighting.

One of Louis's pupils at CFS was his younger brother Ben, who joined the RFC from Sandhurst. The youngster idolised Louis, and it looked as though his dearest wish to emulate his brother's flying feats would be realised, for he proved to be another natural pilot. To increase the skills that would help to keep Ben alive in the hostile skies above the Front, Louis held him as an instructor at Upavon until the inevitable orders came – to join No. 40 Squadron and its SE-5s on the Western Front. Ben was overjoyed. SE-5s! Great show!

Whilst at Upavon, the brothers sometimes flew together to Spetisbury, to land in the fields above the farm and spend an

Louis Strange's young brother Ben shared his love of farming and flying. Unlike Louis, Ben would not survive the war (*Photo: Vecta Mitchell*)

afternoon at home. They flew down to attend the wedding of their sister Stephanie, serving as Officer Commanding Women's Auxiliary Air Force (WAAF) Transport at Salisbury. Their other two sisters were nursing, one in Russia, the other as Commandant of a voluntary hospital in England. Eldest brother Ronald was serving at sea, as he was to do throughout the war with only two brief periods of leave in England. He survived the sinking of HMS *Ocean* in the Dardanelles; commanded one of the first drifters to carry troops into Suvla Bay during the Gallipoli landings; and later commanded a group of mine-sweepers in the Adriatic. The Strange family was living up to its warrior traditions.

Despite his constant pleas for a return to France, Louis was given yet another job within Home Establishment. Shortly after the Royal Flying Corps and the Royal Naval Air Service were integrated into an independent Service called the Royal Air Force (RAF) on the 1st of April 1918 – an occasion hardly noticed by the fliers themselves – Louis Strange was posted to the command of No. 23 (Training) Wing, with responsibility for flying training within Northern Brigade.

One of his first duties was to escort King George and Queen Mary round the aeroplane hangers and airship sheds of the new RAF training base at Cranwell. He flew from Waddington in his Bristol Scout, to find Cranwell completely obscured by mist. He landed in a field, walked three muddy miles across country, and arrived just in time to clean his shoes and be introduced to Their Majesties by a despairing Brigadier General Briggs.

Of far greater importance to Louis Strange than Royal visits were the problems facing him at No. 23 Wing. He considered both the output and the quality of trained pilots to be far too low. By applying the lessons learnt at CFS and Gosport; by unofficially converting his best pupils into instructors as he had done with No. 23 Squadron, and by making optimum use of his own resources rather than waste time demanding external support, Louis Strange within two months more than doubled the Wing's flying hours. His improvements to training techniques and standards reduced the rate of aircraft crashes from one in every thirty hours of flying to one in every sixty hours.

It was again a job to which he applied himself with ingenuity and energy, but with little pleasure. He wanted to be at the Front, not on an airfield in Lincolnshire.

When Louis had left CFS, General Ludlow Hewitt as General Officer Commanding Headquarters Training Brigade had promised that he would continue to press for an operational appointment for the frustrated warrior. But operational posts for Lieutenant Colonels were rare, and had General Hewitt himself not been sent to France to command 10th Brigade, it is likely that Louis Strange would have seen out the war in Home Establishment.

However, on 26th June 1918 he received twenty-four hours' notice to proceed to France, where he was to command the newly formed 80th Wing, under General Ludlow Hewitt.

CHAPTER SIX

Return to Battle

The aerial war to which Louis Strange returned in 1918 was vastly different from the one he had left almost three years before. Practically the only thing that hadn't changed was the arena over which the war in the air was being waged. During those three years and at brutal cost the Front had been edged forwards and backwards no more than a few miles. From the air, the trench lines and the strips of ravaged earth between and behind them reached across Belgium and France like the broad track of some foul and destructive monster.

The men in the air, with a twist of the neck at 10,000 feet and on a clear day, could take some solace from a distant view of England's southern coasts. However, it wouldn't do for them to dwell too long on the sight lest the dry and deadly stutter of gunfire take them by surprise, for as Louis Strange and others had foreseen, the machine-gun now ruled the skies.

No longer were guns added to an aeroplane as an optimistic afterthought; fighter planes were now built around the guns, for no other purpose than to provide them with a powerful, manoeuvrable platform. By June 1918 the techniques, the weaponry and the sheer number of potential targets in the skies could provide fighter pilots like Major Billy Bishop with twenty-five kills in twelve days. Those who wielded their guns to such effect had become the aces of the war: fliers like Von Richthofen, Udet, Guynemer, Fonk, Rickenbacker, Ball, Mannock, McCudden, Bishop. Their 'scores' were applauded by their respective publics like those of competing sportsmen. But there was nothing sporting about death in the air. If the bullets or the shrapnel didn't kill a man outright, death came by fall or flame, for there were no parachutes for Allied fliers throughout the war, and for the Germans only during the final months.

Technical supremacy in the air had seesawed throughout the war, tilted slightly in Germany's favour, partly through British insistence on sending men to likely death in obsolescent aircraft such as the RE-8 and BE-2c, which were still being flown into battle in 1917. Germany also gained advantage through its concentration of experienced pilots into Jastas, the famed 'circuses' of the Western Front, and by placing greater emphasis on aerial combat than on direct ground support. On the other hand the RFC and now the RAF, under Trenchard's aggressive guidance, had never lost sight of the primary purpose of the aerial arm: the support of the land battle. Reconnaissance remained the primary role, but by 1918 greater emphasis had also been given to direct ground support. Low-level bombing and strafing, as pioneered by Louis Strange and his colleagues in 1915, had become an integral part of any ground offensive, and a counter to enemy attack. For the Allies, the role of the fighter was firstly to provide a protective umbrella for these fundamental tasks; the deliberate seeking of enemy aircraft through offensive patrolling was a secondary role.

This offensive policy, with its emphasis on hazardous low-level flying and its deliberate choice of enemy territory as the main arena for aerial warfare, often attracted sickening losses, which may have given the impression to those only interested in scores that the Allies were losing the battle in the air. Far from it. Below its screen of protective fighters and well publicised aces, the RAF was winning that battle by carrying out its primary functions of reconnaissance and tactical support – regardless of loss.

Appropriately, it was to lead a Wing designed for integrated tactical strike that Louis Strange returned to France. Under his command were the SE-5s of Nos 2 and 4 Squadrons of the Australian Flying Corps; the Camels of No. 46; the DH-9s of No. 103, and the Bristol Fighters of No. 88. Nos 92 and 54 Squadrons would later be added to his strength. Under Louis Strange this was to prove a formidable force.

He returned to the Front at a time when the battle was turning in favour of the Allies. The desperate offensive launched by the Germans in March had almost punched a decisive hole in the French and British line. Dogged defence on the ground and in the air had finally stemmed the German advance just short of Amiens. Now, in July, the main counter-attack was being prepared. The role of 80th Wing in this decisive phase of the war would be to reconnoitre the battlefield; to give direct support to Allied ground attacks; and to strike at enemy communications and bases behind the lines. German airfields would become a prime target, in pursuance of the British belief that although the impressive tallies of aircraft shot down by Allied aces made good news at home, it would be more cost effective to destroy those aircraft on the ground or even in the making. While the 'tactical' formations, such as 80th Wing, struck at enemy bases, the RAF's newly formed Independent Force of long-range 'strategic' bombers would attack Germany's manufacturing capacity and morale.

Although heavily involved in the administration of his Wing and in the planning of its operations, Louis Strange flew almost every day to visit his Squadrons and, whenever he could, to join them on offensive patrols or bombing missions. He was well aware that he was flying in a different war from the one he had left three years earlier. Too many of his former colleagues had returned to battle with more zest than good sense and had paid the price, so he flew his early sorties like a novice, with good men around him. But although he didn't go looking for trouble, he soon found it . . .

Seeking to join up with a patrol of No. 46 Squadron Camels, he was a mile distant from them when, in the words of his log, he 'got thoroughly sat upon by four Fokkers'. He pulled out every trick in his aerobatic repertoire to keep them from his tail and snapped off a quick burst of bullets from his twin Vickers whenever a plane came into his line of fire. One disappeared. He was too busy to notice if he had destroyed it. He saw a second dive away and head east. He was still battling with the other two when a Bristol Fighter suddenly appeared on the scene to give him a hand. After a quick exchange of fire the Fokkers made off. That was when Louis Strange made his only mistake. From above the 'Brisfit' he dived down to wave his thanks to his rescuers. He was met with a burst of fire from the observer's rear-mounted Lewis gun. Bullets ripped through the Camel's fuselage and out through the top-plane. His instrument panel disintegrated. He whipped the Camel down and beneath the other machine and high-tailed it back to base. It had been his fault. He had come out of the sun and in the frightened eyes of a young observer the swooping shape could have been a Fokker. Almost twenty years later Louis Strange would meet the leader of the German foursome, who was by coincidence the commander of one of the 80th Wing's opposing formations from across the lines. Von Leutzer was able to confirm that Louis had destroyed one of the four and damaged another. He also recalled how intrigued he had been as he broke away from the battle to see the British aeroplanes disappearing to the west, apparently fighting each other . . .

That was a rare mistake. Louis Strange, although a fearless flier, was not a foolish one. 'To hell with the consequences' was a philosophy for the desk, not the cockpit, in which he always tempered boldness with discretion and encouraged his men to do likewise. He shared the view of British ace James McCudden 'that the correct way to wage war is to down as many as possible of the enemy at the least risk, expense, and casualties to one's own side'. [1]

Louis Strange applied this philosophy to his own combat flying, to his training of others and to his planning of operations. As the commander of a Wing he was particularly anxious to ensure that those engaged in bombing and reconnaissance should have adequate protection from enemy fighters. By a radical re-design of bombing and escort tactics he quickly increased the success rate and decreased the losses within his Squadrons, at no extra cost in flying hours. A priceless bonus was an improvement in morale, particularly within No. 103 Squadron, whose unescorted DH-9s had previously suffered heavily when attacked over their targets. Now, with their raids planned to overlap with the offensive patrols of the Wing's Fighter Squadrons, they enjoyed almost constant cover. No doubt there were those entirely aggressive spirits in the Fighter Squadrons, and particularly amongst the Australians, who would rather have been chasing the Hun instead of waiting for him to come to them as they flew 'top cover', but they soon saw the sense of their Wing Commander's policy of integrating the Squadrons. This reached its peak in the series of full Wing operations launched by Louis Strange, beginning in August.

The Wing had seen fierce action in support of the Allied offensive on 8th August, which Von Ludendorff would later describe as the 'black day of the German Army'. Although the front line before Amiens was only pushed back some 11 miles, the blow to German morale was devastating. The tide had turned. As the Allied advance drew breath and the demands for direct air support lessened, Louis Strange, encouraged by General Ludlow Hewitt, prepared to launch his whole Wing in integrated attacks on enemy airfields. He allocated tasks and timings to each of his Squadrons, whose aircraft were concentrated into one massive tactical strike-force. The first attack was on Von Leutzer's aerodrome at Haubourdin on 15th August. Louis Strange didn't just plan the raid; he flew on the wing-tip of its leader, Captain A H ('Harry') Cobby, who with twenty-four confirmed kills would finish the war as Australia's most decorated and successful fighter ace. Under a protective top cover of No. 92 Squadron's SE-5s and No. 88's Bristol Fighters, the Camels of the Australian Squadrons and the DH-9s of No. 103 unleashed 150 bombs and 20,000 rounds of machine-gun fire upon Haubourdin's aircraft, hangers, billets, workshops and fuel-dumps from a height of some 200 feet. The airfield was devastated. All 65 of Louis Strange's aircraft returned safely to their fields.

While his Squadrons celebrated into the early hours, Louis Strange prepared another raid for the following day. Harry Cobby recalled how he was woken from two hours of sleep by a batman with a 'bracer' and a couple of aspirins for breakfast, and the news that another Wing 'show' had been ordered. He pulled his flying-gear on over his pyjamas and staggered out to his aircraft, which had its upper wing-surface painted white to signify his status as leader. Other squadrons were already gathering overhead. Nobody knew where they were going until Louis Strange arrived with an aerial photograph of Lomme airfield, the base of the famous Boelcke Jagdstaffel, now led by Lieutenant Bolle. Louis handed the photograph to Cobby. 'All yours,' he said, and climbed into his own Camel. Cobby commented:

> I don't think anyone else in the air, with the exception of Strange, knew where we were going. The colonel had again tucked himself in just behind my left wing-tip, too close this morning for comfort, and I said enough to burn the dope off his wing. I made up my mind that if he wanted excitement he would get it. Instead, therefore, of coming in as low as we had the previous day, I stayed up a thousand feet or so and then pushed into an almost vertical dive that nearly bucked me through the centre section . . . [2]

Louis Strange takes up the story:

> Down we went with every wire screaming protest. I pressed the triggers of my Constantinesco gear as I saw the tracer bullets stream out in front of the bull-like nose of his Camel, and a second later thought I was bound to crash vertically into the roof of the hanger below us, which was one of six.
>
> As we flattened out and streaked over those hangars, I tugged hard at the release thongs of my bomb gear, and then heard the most awful din of crashes when the whole of the Flight sent down their total of twenty-four 20-lb bombs. The next good look I had at Lomme showed

Sopwith F-1 Camel of No. 46 Squadron with bombs installed under the fuselage. It was in this type of plane that Louis Strange flew with his Wing on tactical strikes against German airfields and communications in 1918 (*Photo: Jack Bruce*)

me all the six hangars enveloped in black smoke clouds, edged with reddish-yellow flames that poured out on the windward side. Anti-aircraft bursts seemed to be all over the air from a hundred feet upwards, for the Hun had been wise enough after his experience at Haubourdin to rush all his available Archies to Lomme. All the same our machines suffered very little damage from their attentions, although some of them, which came down as low as fifty feet off the ground to drop their bombs, got a bit knocked about by the concussions set up by the bursting of those same *eggs*. [3]

Both Haubourdin and Lomme were subsequently abandoned.

One who flew with Louis Strange on later and even larger tactical strikes of this nature was Major Coningham, commanding No. 92 Squadron. In the next world war he would become one of the greatest exponents of close air support in his command of tactical air forces in North Africa and Europe. It was, he would state, Louis Strange who had taught him the effective use of fighter-bombers under a canopy of air superiority; who had taught him the basics of ground attack, such as destroying the head of a column first, then the rear, then the immobilised mass between; whose 'high influence and unequalled leadership' had made such an effective force of the 80th Wing.

This opinion was evidently shared by Ludlow Hewitt, who in the space of two months nominated Louis Strange for the Distinguished Service Order (DSO) and the Distinguished Flying Cross (DFC) for his planning of and participation in the large-scale tactical strikes. Both were awarded.

During August and again in early September of 1918 Louis was able to fly into Bryas aerodrome to lunch with young Ben. He found his brother bubbling with enthusiasm, proud of the successes he had already achieved with 40 Squadron. He was, according to his Squadron Commander, a gifted and fearless pilot, and the life and soul of the Mess. On his second visit, Louis found that Ben had been promoted to Flight Commander. Such early advancement was due partly to the skills that had already brought his number of confirmed victories to five, but due also to the heavy losses sustained by 40 Squadron. Sensing that Ben might be over-anxious to avenge the death of too many friends, Louis tried to impart some of his constructive caution to the spirited youngster before he clapped him on the shoulder and flew back to his own part of the war.

Louis Strange had a soft spot for his Australian Squadrons, and immense admiration for their leaders: fliers like Majors Murray Jones and McCloughry, Captain King, and Harry Cobby, on whose wing-tip he so often flew. The respect was mutual, although tempered on the part of the Australians with some exasperation. Cobby, who had a preference for pre-dawn solo flights over enemy lines in search of yawning Huns, said this of Louis Strange:

> One of the doubtful privileges that we were granted in No. 4 was that of looking after the machines of both the Brigade Commander and the Wing Commander. Brigadier Ludlow Hewitt used his Camel mainly for visits to the different units under his command. The Wing Commander, Colonel Louis Strange, was in a different category. He was one of those likeable energetic personalities and no matter how busy the job was of administering the Wing, he could always find time to dash along and demand his machine. My greatest complaint was that no matter how much fighting we had been doing he was always eager that I should pick one or two other chaps and take him over the lines to have a look at this, that, or the other. He was one of those persons with more than the average issue of guts. All he wanted was to be let loose in any old sort of trouble at all. I used to devote a lot of time to studying where one met with the most 'hate' so that Strange would get a bellyful next time he wanted to go out! He was a grand type, both as a man and a leader of flying people. [2]

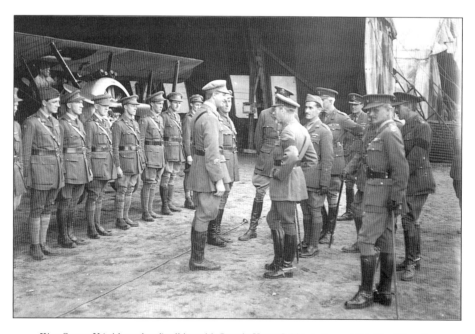

King George V (with armband) talking with Captain Harry Cobby during a visit to No. 4 Squadron. Immediately to the right of the King is the Squadron Commander, Major McCloughry. Louis Strange is centre background of the visiting group

As a countryman himself, Louis Strange related the flying skills of the Australians, and particularly their pathfinding abilities, to their 'outback' traditions.

> In individual squadron fighting those Australians had no equals in their best days, and more than once they raised the record for the numbers of enemy aircraft destroyed in one day by any one squadron. The secret of their success was, in my opinion, mainly due to their sense of initiative, which they inherited from ancestors who had been cattlemen, sheep-ranchers, poachers, trappers, outriders . . . In fact, Nos 2 and 4 Squadrons were masters in the art of guerilla warfare. [3]

On the other hand, such initiative and the guerilla instinct could bring embarrassment upon a Wing Commander . . .

> It might have been insulting to hint at cattle-stealing ancestry, but when we others were existing on tinned milk, the Australians always had their own fresh milk from their own cows and a lorry to transport the cows whenever a move had to be made. Moreover these cows always had calves with great regularity. Of course it would have been bad form to question the origin of the new piano, the cows and the calves which they invited a Wing Commander to see. These accessories meant so much to the amenity of their life on the ground, and so the Wing Commander could only let them get away with it, even though he knew it was his pigeon if anyone raised awkward inquiries. [3]

It was the nature of Louis Strange's leadership to give his Australians, and others under his command, as much slack rope as he could; even at the risk of hanging himself.

He was a firm supporter of the 'fight hard and play hard' creed born in the early days of the RFC and now becoming an established tradition of the young RAF. Indeed, youthful and sometimes eccentric exuberance was a tradition of flight itself; hadn't Louis Strange himself been a hearty participant at that 'Upside Down Dinner' of 1913? Now, as a leader of combat fliers he recognised the need to submerge fear, release tension, celebrate success. And if staid Army colleagues commented on what they might consider the excessively boisterous nature of RAF Guest Nights, Louis Strange, if he wasn't himself dancing on the piano or buried in the scrummage on the carpet, would likely tell them what to do with such stuffy opinions.

On the morning of 24th September Louis Strange received an urgent message from the Commanding Officer of No. 40 Squadron. Young Ben had not returned from the dawn patrol. Louis flew down to

71

Bryas. He was told that in fierce dogfighting Ben had destroyed one Hun before another was seen to latch onto his tail. His SE-5 had tumbled earthwards, apparently out of control, and was last seen spinning into the mist far below.

'Poor old Ben missing. Must hope for the best, but feel there's no chance. Cannot describe my feelings for Mother and Father,' Louis scrawled in his log-book at the end of that long day. [4]

Later he would say:

> As I tried to write a letter home that night a real hatred of the whole business came over me for the first time in all those four years of war. I cannot say that I hated the Hun, although I knew from now onward to the finish I would fight and destroy far more relentlessly than ever. I just hated the ghastly waste of war. I could only try to console myself by the thought that Ben had gone to join all those other good friends of his and mine. He must have gone without knowing what had happened to him or how it had happened, so that his last moments were those of exultation at having got another blighter good and hearty . . . [3]

The following day he flew out over the lines 'feeling desperate to get something back for Ben'. [4] All he could find was a German observation balloon on which to vent his fury. Whenever he could during the following weeks, from the air and on the ground, he scoured the battlefield over which Ben had disappeared. 'Flew round Cambrai low down to see if I could see anything of Ben's machine. Ground very much smashed about. Couldn't see anything,' he wrote on 7th October. [4]

There would be no more 'good hunting', no more 'great show', no more 'fine sport' in that log-book. For the few remaining weeks of the war it would be a brusque record of his sorties, with occasional cries of harsh triumph.

'Low bombing attack on Tournai. Ammunition train blown up . . .'

'Got a Fokker biplane, shot him off a DH-9's tail . . .'

'80th Wing broke all records, 32 Huns destroyed in one day . . .' [4]

He made no comment in his *Recollections* nor in his log-book of the incident that was quoted in the citation for his DSO:

> By his fine example and inspiring personal influence he has raised his wing to still higher efficiency and morale, the enthusiasm displayed by the various squadrons for low-flying raids being most marked. On Oct. 30th he accompanied one of these raids against an aerodrome; watching the work of his machines, he waited until they had finished then dropped his bombs from 100 feet altitude on hangars that were undamaged, then

attacked troops and transport in the vicinity of the aerodrome. Whilst thus engaged he saw eight Fokkers flying above him; at once he climbed and attacked them single handed: having driven one down out of control he was fiercely engaged by the other seven, but he maintained the combat until rescued by a patrol of our scouts.

By that time the Germany Army was being forced back across the shell-pocked land they had taken during their spring offensive, back to and then beyond the old battlefields around Cambrai. The Wing played its part in keeping the pressure on the retreating foe, striking behind the lines at his columns, his communications, his airfields and above all at his morale. Louis Strange put together eighty planes for a Wing assault on Tournai, and almost a hundred virtually to destroy the enemy on Rebaix airfield. German pilots still fought with an almost desperate spirit, but were now being outflown by the new Sopwith Snipes of the British fighter squadrons. And there were fewer Huns in the air. Shortage of fuel, lack of replacements and the destruction of machines on their airfields were thinning their numbers. On the ground, the German retreat became a rout. The straggling grey columns presented easy targets. 'Many lorries burnt and destroyed by direct hits, many casualties caused amongst massed troops on the roads, great havoc and confusion caused to horse transport, guns, etc.,' noted Louis Strange in his log. [4] Moving up behind the Allied advance, his Squadrons occupied airfields recently abandoned by their opposing Jastas.

On 9th November the Wing attack on Enghien airfield was led by Major Maxwell of No. 54 Squadron, with Louis Strange in his slipstream. There was little opposition.

On 10th November Louis Strange flew alongside Major Murray Jones and his Australians, whose turn it was to lead the Wing even deeper into enemy territory to strike at an already beaten foe.

On 11th November he was woken at 2 a.m. It was an Orderly with a message. It was marked 'Urgent'.

'Hostilities will cease at 1100 today . . . Patrols . . . should not operate further forward than the line of our balloons.'

Louis Strange gave instructions for the message to be sent to his Squadrons. 'Then I turned over and went to sleep again, dimly wondering what on earth we were going to do with ourselves in the morning without a war.' [3]

What he did in the morning was to wake early and drive to the Australians' airfield at Grand Ennetières, where his Camel was kept, thinking that he might take one last flight over the lines before peace broke out. And he might as well take a few bombs . . .

"C" Form.
MESSAGES AND SIGNALS.

Army Form C. 2123
(In books of 100.)

No. of Message _____

Prefix 16 Code 084 Words 58	Received.	Sent, or sent out.	Office Stamp.
£ s. d.	From _____	At _____ m.	
Charges to Collect	By _____	To	
Service Instructions _Urgent_		By _____	

Handed in at __KBD__   Office __0845__ m   Received __0850__ m

TO   **80 Wing**

*Sender's Number 96	Day of Month. 11	In reply to Number	A A A

HOSTILITIES will cease at 1100
today aaa No operations should be
undertaken which cannot be
completed by that hour
and no machines will
cross the lines after
that hour aaa Patrols
will be maintained but
should not operate further
forward than the line
of our balloons

FROM
PLACE & TIME   Operations RAf adv GHQ
via 10 Bde

* This line should be erased if not required.

0310—W.14832—100,000—2/17—E.P.Co.—(E930.)

The message to cease hostilities, received by Louis Strange on 11th November 1918

74

80 Wing R.A.F. Squadron	1ST JULY TO 11TH NOV. 1918.				BALLOON
	IN FLAMES.	CRASHED.	O.O.C.	DRIVEN DOWN.	DESTROYED
4 A.F.C.	19	57	36	7	22
88	20	33	53	15	
2 A.F.C	10	30	48	16	
92	4	15	8	1	
103	5	12	30	3	
46	3	11	5	4	1
54	2	2			
TOTALS	63	160	180	46	23

The 80th Wing scoreboard shows numbers of enemy aircraft destroyed in the air, but does not show those destroyed on the ground by the Squadrons primarily engaged in bombing, nor does it indicate the importance of the Wing's reconnaissance and ground-strafing roles. OOC means 'out of control'

It appeared that this thought had occurred to every other flier. They all wanted a last go at the Hun. There wasn't a serviceable machine on the ground. Even his own had been 'borrowed'. Someone had taken it up to test the guns for him, a red-faced Flight Sergeant lied. Louis drove on to his other airfields. They too were empty.

> About 11 a.m., pilots started coming back, and shortly afterwards we got another message through to the effect that the Armistice had been signed and hostilities had ceased at 11 a.m. I was not quite so sure about this last point, because when I questioned several of the Australian pilots, they said they had not seen any balloons, and asked most innocently how far east the balloon line was supposed to be. But I noticed that their bomb-racks were empty. [3]

The following morning, sucking in draughts of cold air at 2,000 feet to clear his head of the previous night's celebrations, Lieutenant Colonel Louis Strange, DSO, MC, DFC and mentioned three times in despatches, flew his battle-scarred Camel to England, there to hold his two-month-old son Brian for the first time.

CHAPTER SEVEN

Spartan Times

After two weeks of unaccustomed tranquillity at Sutton Scotney with Marjorie and their child, Louis Strange returned to France, recording that 'a following wind took me back to Lille in just over two hours.' Can one sense a sigh of relief at being back in the air? Celebrations were still in full swing. In Lille, they reached their height when King George V, with the Prince of Wales and the Duke of York, attended a show by Leslie Henson's 5th Army Concert Party. Of this visit Louis wrote:

> Afterwards the two Princes came to our mess and kept a wonderful party going until 3 a.m., saying when they left that they 'would have to be careful not to wake up father when they got back to the hotel'. Having bidden them goodnight long ago, that august personage fondly imagined them sound asleep in bed. [1]

The last task for 80th Wing before it was disbanded at the end of January was to collect German aircraft for disposal – and to fly them a lot further than was necessary, with both professional interest and a certain feeling of dreamlike disbelief as they peered out over the cowlings of Albatross and Fokker and Rumpler.

On the 1st of February 1919 Louis flew back to England to attend a dinner at the Savoy Hotel 'In Honour of the Squadrons of the RNAS and the RFC which went overseas August 1914'. The survivors of that band of adventurers were greatly outnumbered by the guests. Afterwards, Louis felt dreadfully ill. He thought it might have been the haggis that had followed the *Roulade Farci aux Marrons*. It wasn't the haggis. It was the Spanish flu that had swept through Europe in 1918 and returned that winter to kill more people than had died in the war. It almost killed Louis Strange.

He survived, and although not fully recovered he returned to Belgium within a month to command 51st Wing. His Headquarters was close to the field of Waterloo, in the Château Lillois. There he was made welcome by the Comte and Comtesse de Meuss and their small daughter Jacqueline, who looked upon 'Le Colonel Strange' as their personal saviour from German occupation.

The Wing was equipped almost entirely with Bristol Fighters which were, said Louis:

magnificent machines, and I fancy the hundred hours or so I did in them while commanding the 51st Wing were the most enjoyable I ever experienced, partly perhaps because the four years of war had taught me to appreciate the joys of flying in peace time. [1]

No more Archie. No more squinting over the shoulder for the enemy coming out of the sun. No more head winds draining the fuel from the tanks on the long flight back from the bombing and strafing runs.

Those hundred hours in Bristol Fighters were only briefly recorded in his log-book. More prominence was given to the Wing golf handicap, which he won with rounds of 72 and 70, and to the steeplechase races in which he rode, usually on the Boisfort course: 'Unplaced on SPLASH 3 times, fell twice. Unplaced once, two 3rds and one 2nd on AERIAL POST. Fell when leading by 7 or 8 lengths a furlong from the post. Two jolly good horses . . .' [2]

He also flew back to England that summer to shoot at Bisley for the King's Cup.

In June, the Wing moved to Spich, a former Zeppelin base, with the Wing Headquarters at Bad Godesberg on the Rhine. It was fine country for both flying and riding, but Louis was not sorry when 51st Wing was also disbanded and he returned to England, to command Gosport and Andover for brief periods before taking up the post of Chief Flying Instructor at CFS, still at Upavon.

From there he soon moved to command the Flying Wing of RAF Cadet College Cranwell, under Air Marshal Charles Longcroft. It was perhaps the most prestigious flying appointment in the Service. Through his hands passed many of the young fliers destined to lead the RAF into a second world war. Dermot Boyle, one of the first, and Louis's Administrative Officer, Squadron Leader Portal, were both to become Marshals of the Royal Air Force. In such a post, with an outstanding war record and now holding a permanent commission in the RAF, Louis Strange too seemed to have all the qualifications to advance to high rank. Perhaps he might have done. Or perhaps his impatience with red tape, his fierce independence and his non-conformist spirit would not have attracted favour and promotion in a more restrictive peacetime Air Force. We shall never know. Through-out 1921 he was in poor health. The strains of 1,000 hours of wartime flying, more than half of them in combat conditions, had been heightened by a weakness left from the near-fatal bout of peritonitis in 1916 and the recent attack of influenza, and had left him subject to sciatica, insomnia and recurrent bouts of depression and physical debility. Like many who had fought and flown throughout the war, his body and his mind needed rest. He could have found it behind

Louis Strange, with Marjorie, after receiving his first Distinguished Flying Cross at Buckingham Palace in 1922

RAF desks, but that was not his style. Medical and family advice pointed him gently towards retirement. Towards a break from flying. Towards the land.

In early 1992 Louis Strange took that advice, and a small disability pension.

78

Because the RAF at that time did not promulgate retired ranks, he resigned his commission in the junior Service and retired as a Lieutenant Colonel in the Dorsetshire Regiment. 'Colonel Louis', as he was to be known in the civilian world that he now rejoined, turned back to his first love. The land.

In 1916, John Strange had left the valley of the Stour to buy and farm 1,300 acres at Worth Matravers on the Isle of Purbeck. He bought buildings and land for £11,000 and could have bought the village too for a little more. The land was in bad heart, the water supply poor and the farm buildings in a dreadful state. But John Strange noted the size of the thistles and the luxuriance of the clover in the pathways between the exhausted fields, and knew that with careful husbandry he could restore the land to health. His workforce went with him: George Studley, Steve Marchment, Ned and William Fiander, and Sidney Hopkins. They drove his fifty-five dairy cows and heifers by easy stages the 30 miles to Worth, and set about the conversion of poor arable land and thistly grazing to a flourishing dairy farm.

To help John Strange in early 1922 came his two surviving sons, Louis and Ronald. Just as ill health had forced Louis out of the air, so it had caused Ronald to abandon a promising career at sea. After almost continuous active service he had left the Royal Navy with every prospect of taking a ship of his own in the Union Castle Line, but had

In 1922 'Colonel Louis' (seated third from left) returned to farming – and to play for the Corfe cricket team. On Louis's left is Doctor Drury, team captain (*Photo: David Strange*)

79

failed the medical exam because of damage to his eardrums from naval gunfire. So the two young 'disabled veterans' of the First World War joined their father at Worth Matravers, and applied themselves with a will to the older man's farming philosophy: 'Work as if you are going to die tomorrow. And farm as if you were going to live forever. Trust in providence, but hoe between the rows.' [3]

Hard work it was. There were barns to be converted into cottages for the families of the two brothers; new dairy buildings to be completed; arable fields to be grassed down; new stock to be bought in; the cliff-edge to be fenced along the southern boundary; concrete reservoirs to be laid at the springs, and a 10,000-gallon tank from a tramp steamer to be adapted to water storage. A year of drought and a drop of two-thirds in the selling price of milk by 1925 severely tested the industry and spirit of the Strange family. They re-opened an old stone quarry, began cheese-making and set up their own shop in Swanage to market their dairy produce. These initiatives saw them through the bad times. Also, John Strange's long-term policy of land-improvement began to take effect. By the autumn of 1928 they had 400 head of cattle and 57 good ricks of hay, some retained from the previous year, which had always been John Strange's aim. 'You should always have one year's hay in hand,' he used to say, 'for old ricks, like stale bread, last twice as long as the new ones.' [3]

Also by 1928 Louis Strange's other love was calling to him again. Seven years of farming had restored his health. 'Hard work close to mother earth is a certain cure for most ills, and a farmer's life is a good one provided you are not interested in making a lot of money,' he wrote. [1] Now he wanted to return to flying.

Ronald, who had not been through the same youthful apprenticeship on the land that Louis had experienced at Lower Almer, was by now a competent farmer, and the farm itself was in good fettle. It no longer needed Louis. He decided to return to flying as a career. With some misgivings, but knowing better than to try to dissuade him, the family accepted his decision. It was not the first time, nor would it be the last, that Louis put flying before family. But in what capacity would he go back to the air?

Although he had flown infrequently since leaving the RAF, he had followed with interest the development of aviation since 1921. It is likely that during the first four years of his retirement from the Service he would have been disappointed at the slow pace of such development, particularly in Britain. The peacetime RAF, understandably reduced in strength, had been forced to fight for its life against the efforts of the Army and Navy to dismember the upstart and take control of their own air support. The energy and foresight of

Trenchard, as Chief of the Air Staff, had saved the junior Service, but financial stringency had muffled technical advance. The biplane fighters and wire-festooned bombers of 1925 differed little from those of 1918. In civil aviation, the immediate and boisterous post-war confidence in commercial air services had foundered in the face of economic decline and lack of Government subsidies. A handful of adventurers had established pioneer airlines and contract flying services, but the competition was strong and the rewards were lean.

But from 1925, Louis Strange would have sensed a growing excitement in the air. It was born not of public opinion and certainly not of Government support, but of the efforts of individual designers and fliers. The sleek, single-winged seaplanes of the Schneider Trophy races would certainly have tugged at his heart-strings. He would have admired the well publicised long-distance flights of Alan Cobham in Geoffrey De Havilland's biplanes, and Byrd's flight to the North Pole in a new tri-motored monoplane built by Fokker. He would have approved the beauty of the Southampton flying-boats, and would probably have muttered 'about time too' when the Bulldog and the Siskin appeared with RAF roundels over an all-metal framework. He would have read with a touch of nostalgia the reports of the annual RAF display at Hendon, scene of his own ragtime flying. In 1927 he would have applauded the bravery and skill of a young American called Charles Lindbergh, and might have seen in the public acclaim accorded to this first solo flight over the Atlantic some return to the heady spirit that had greeted the early days of powered flight. Was a new golden age of flight about to dawn? He sensed that it was. And he wanted to be part of it.

He had followed with particular interest the progress of light-aircraft construction, and of the racing and club-flying associated with it. Five state-aided clubs had been established in Britain by 1926, and three more added by 1928. Others were planned, and the number of private clubs was growing steadily. Louis had even tried to start a flying club at Worth Matravers, where he built a small hanger on the football field. The project had failed through lack of support, but it was here at club level, he believed, that the immediate future of aviation lay, in the development of flying as a source of international friendship rather than international conflict, and in the design and production of light aircraft at low cost. It was towards this field of aviation that in 1928 he directed his revived enthusiasm for flight.

He sought advice from Charles Grey, the respected and often outspoken editor of *Aeroplane* and a friend of Louis since they had dined together at that 'Upside Down Dinner' in early 1913. He told him of his plans to set up an Isle of Purbeck flying club, to become involved in the development of light aeroplanes, but first of all to buy one for himself. He had piloted several of the new breed of light aircraft, and although he had noted little advance in airframe construction, he had been excited by the vast increase in power and reliability that came from the improvements in engine and airscrew design. Should he buy a De Havilland? One of the new Cirrus Moths? De Havilland had certainly captured the bulk of the light-aircraft market, and his various Moths had won Britain's première air race, the King's Cup, in 1926 and 1927. But there were other companies, Charles Grey reminded him, smaller companies, with whom it might be easier for Louis Strange to gain a position of some influence. He might, Charles Grey suggested, care to take a look at a promising new design by a man called Oliver Simmonds . . .

Oliver Simmonds had left his job with the Southampton-based Supermarine company in March 1928 to construct an aircraft of his own design. It was to be a two-seater biplane, with a unique feature: Its major components would be interchangeable. This would reduce the cost of production, and of subsequent maintenance. It could be the cheapest plane of its type.

Simmonds wanted to have the machine ready for the King's Cup race in July. That gave him just four months to build and test it. With a skilled woodworker called Thomas Hiett and several part-time workers from the Supermarine factory, he made the fuselage in the lounge and the wings in the bedrooms of his home in Woolston, Southampton. When the main components were completed, he removed the front door and the window-frames of his house to get them out. The prototype was assembled in a former munitions factory called the Rolling Mills. The machine had a symmetrical wing section which allowed all the main planes and ailerons to be interchangeable. Either side of the tailplane could be changed with the other or with the fin and rudder. All main bracing wires were identical, as were the two undercarriage legs. It was powered by a 95-hp HDC Cirrus-3 engine, to give an ample reserve of power to lift the biplane out of the small private airfields for which it was intended. Oliver Simmonds called his aircraft a Spartan.

When ready for flight the prototype was towed with folded wings to a field at Bartlock Heath. It was a small field. Coming in to land after a flight of some twenty minutes in the expert hands of Flight Lieutenant Webster of the RAF High Speed Flight at Calshot, the plane over-ran the landing area and nosed into a ditch, damaging fuselage and propeller.

But Simmonds had it repaired and painted in race livery for the King's Cup just a few weeks later. Webster flew it in the race, and although the Spartan finished well down the field, the fact that the untried machine finished at all was to its credit. Oliver Simmonds decided to put the Spartan into production, and submitted papers for the formation of Simmonds Aircraft Ltd.

It was at this stage that Louis Strange came to see him. Louis liked the man, and he liked his aeroplane. He was impressed by the concept of interchangeable components and the low cost of production, purchase and maintenance. He particularly liked the roomy luggage compartment: space enough for golf-clubs! He borrowed the aircraft for a series of test-flights and liked it even more. This was the plane and the company for him. In August, he joined Oliver Simmonds as co-director, principal salesman and chief test pilot of Simmonds Aircraft Ltd.

One of his first acts was to take the Spartan to his field at Worth Matravers where, in company with two De Havilland Moths, he mounted a flying show 'to stimulate interest in the science of flying and to attract membership to the Swanage and Isle of Purbeck Light Aeroplane Club', as the local press said. Louis Strange obtained the services of experienced pilot H W R Banting as Chief Flying Instructor for his Purbeck Club.

In October the Spartan prototype showed its true paces when, piloted by Banting, with Louis in the unaccustomed role of passenger, it flew from Croydon to Templehof for the Berlin Air Show in 7 hours 10 minutes. The outbound flight was made in poor visibility and lowering cloud, which forced them to fly at 200 feet by the time they reached Ostend:

> This height enabled us to watch very clearly our friends the Belgians just waking up and taking their morning milk bottles from the doorstep. And then Holland . . . Strips of tulip bed and black and white cows. I also noted that most of the farms possessed a large brown dog . . . By 09.30 most of the high ground was beginning to connect with the clouds, until on reaching the German frontier at Oldenzaal it became necessary to stick right on the railway to Bentheim. Our altimeter showed minus 100 feet from Croydon aerodrome, and there being nothing to see between the clouds and the roof-tops, it occurred to us that a canal, perhaps, would be less likely to enter a tunnel suddenly than a railway . . . The weather began to clear until at Minden we were flying at 3,000 feet in beautiful weather, with a grand view of the Harz Mountains ahead to the SE. This is good flying country, with the names of towns plainly written on the aerodromes, and smoke fires in the circle, and other things comforting to a pilot's eye . . . [4]

And so to Berlin. The return trip seems to have been less interesting, but faster. The time of 5 hours 55 minutes was an unofficial long-distance record for a light aeroplane with passenger.

This performance and the demonstrations that Louis gave at Croydon attracted several orders, and production of the first twelve Spartans began at the Rolling Mills, with a work-force of seventy. The first production machine was completed by the end of the year, and was christened Cirrus-Spartan by the Mayoress of Southampton at a factory ceremony on the 31st of December. The brief speech that 'Colonel Strange' gave before proposing the health of the Mayoress was reported in *Flight*:

> Col. Strange said that in the past our greatness was to some extent built up by encouragement of the sea to protect trade and the country. He thought that this generation should see that it encouraged the spirit of the air. Only by encouraging the youth to fly, and to fly naturally, should we ensure the same great traditions in the future . . . [5]

This belief in the 'spirit of the air' would guide Louis Strange's involvement in civil aviation for the rest of his life.

On the day after its christening, Louis Strange test-flew the first production Spartan from Hamble, where the company now rented a Hangar. Test-flying, demonstration flying, and a vigorous sales campaign became his working life. Charles Grey was later to write, 'Lt. Col. Louis Strange proved himself to be one of the world's finest salesmen of aeroplanes.' In fact he was too good, for he persuaded some companies to order more than they really needed or could afford. Within the first few months of 1929 he took orders for some fifty aircraft. More staff were taken on, and credit was extended to buy materials. The future looked bright. But the early promise began to fade as a number of orders were cancelled, or reduced. The company was left with far too much stock-in-trade. Staff were stood off, and wages for those remaining were cut, but the financial deficit could not be recovered. An injection of capital was essential if the company was to survive. Louis sought his friend Captain Harold Balfour. They had flown together on the Western Front. Now Member of Parliament for Thanet, this former RFC pilot would become Lord Balfour of Inchrye. He persuaded Lord Cowdray's Whitehall Securities Corporation to rescue the ailing company, which was renamed Spartan Aircraft Ltd. Oliver Simmonds left the organisation to become a Member of Parliament, and although Louis Strange remained on the Board of Directors, control now passed to the corporation, which also held a majority holding in Saunders Roe Ltd, based at Cowes. Throughout 1930 there was progressive relocation of Spartan production to the Cowes factory, and the growth of closer relationships with Saunders Roe.

There had been nothing wrong with the Simmonds Spartan. The interchangeability of parts remained a good selling-point, and the sturdiness and reliability of the aircraft was never in doubt. Not everyone, however, favoured wings of symmetrical section, particularly for the aircraft when used in a basic-training role. Now, with the benefit of experience, with more capital available, and with the added design expertise of Sir Alliot Vernon-Roe and his 'Saro' team, improved versions in the form of the Spartan Arrow and the Spartan Three-Seater were soon being test-flown and demonstrated throughout the country by Louis Strange. The new types retained a degree of interchangeability, but the symmetrical wing section was gone. The three-seater became a favoured joy-ride aircraft, the best-known being the Island Queen, operated by Sandown and Shanklin Flying Services, and Helen of Troy, flown at the travelling air circuses throughout Britain by Pauline Gower.

Spartans also flew in most of the air races of the 1930s. Louis Strange himself featured in many of them. It was a good way to demonstrate the aircraft, and above all it was fun, although he gave a wry smile on those occasions when he found himself billed as a 'veteran' of air racing. He flew one of the new Spartan Arrows in the 1930 King's Cup:

> Almost every club in the country had two or three entries and some
> more. At Hanworth that day we met, it seemed, everyone connected
> with club and private flying. It was indeed a gathering of flying friends
> from all over the country, with much more the feeling of a day's sport

Louis Strange test-flying a Spartan seaplane at Hamble in 1932

rather than a race – more like a day's hunting than a point-to-point. That sixty of these ordinary club and private aircraft stood up to 700 miles at full throttle, and that no major accident of any sort was recorded, speaks wonderfully well of the reliability of the engines and quality of flying. Miss Winifred Brown's win was a very popular one and thoroughly well deserved.

My engine ran perfectly up to the Newcastle control and I had been steadily gaining places, but there it refused to start and by the time the fault in the impulse-starting magneto had been tracked and put right, I had lost all and more than the ground I had gained. Another Spartan flown by Flt Lt Gibbons when well placed on the last control, was taxied into by a Moth, and his chance was gone by the time the damaged parts could be replaced . . . Everyone had perfectly good excuses for not winning . . . [6]

A month later one of the Arrows put up a fine performance to finish ninth out of sixty starters in the eight-day Circuit of Europe, and in the 1931 King's Cup, Flight Lieutenant Gibbons flew a Spartan into second place. Louis won none of the major events, but took the trophies and prize-money in several of the lesser handicap and pylon races. He took first places at Nottingham and Leeds in 1930, twice at Blackpool in 1931, and at Skegness and Thanet in 1932. At one of the Blackpool races, an observant reporter for *Flight* noticed that Louis topped up his tanks with a last drop of petrol after he had warmed the engine up, a practice of those who had flown long-range combat missions beyond the Western Front. The prize-money won in these races, usually between fifty and a hundred pounds, he would take to the Spartan factory at Cowes on the following Monday morning and have it distributed amongst the workers, or converted into a barrel of beer. They built the aeroplane; he only had to fly it.

His own writings convey his love of racing and of the flying-club spirit of the 1930s:

Let us suppose that it's Cardiff's day, and we are in one of the competing aircraft. Twenty aircraft of a dozen different types are lined up at Heston. Dancy and Rowarth have done their handicapping, the pilots of the slower machines have started their engines, and Mr Reynolds the starter has his flag up. Away goes the first machine; his speed is about 80 mph, so he gets pretty well half-way to Cardiff, well past Swindon, before the scratch machine doing 160 mph roars away, and there they are, all strung out along the track, but at once the overhauling begins, and round about the high ground of the Cotswolds overlooking the mouth of the River Severn, a spectator would probably be able to see the leading aircraft pegging along right on the water half-way to Cardiff airport from where he was standing, and the last machine just in sight looking towards the east. We are now lying fourth, having gone up two places, and are closing up on the third with two more still ahead; the chimney-stacks of Cardiff's factories are already in sight, but we may still have a chance. The wheels almost make tracks on the mud flats that show up with the tide low, flying against a fair breeze. But we need not have worried about catching up the two in front, for already a slim looking monoplane goes serenely past our slower biplane. The chimney-stacks are close now, we might be third, or even possibly second; we are passing another biplane now, the aerodrome is well in sight and we are only 50 yards behind the next in front . . . now 20 . . . now just level as we cross the boundary of the aerodrome and catch a glimpse of the gaily-coloured crowd all round it . . . yes, we are well into second place with only a hundred yards to go, but . . . whizz . . . whizz . . . a green monoplane to starboard and a red one to port . . . and we have just been beaten out of third place. Twelve aeroplanes cross the finishing line in as many seconds; most of them have beaten themselves by making small errors here and there. Another grand success for the handicappers, Dancy and Rowarth, and a wonderfully exciting finish for the competitors and spectators.

Before and after the finish of the race the crowd has to be kept interested and thrilled or amused, so first a fly-past of the local Auxiliary Air Squadron in close formation goes by, and then the parachutist goes up and does his stuff, and then the comic turn, when a spectator in a top hat and tails is seen rushing out of the crowd to an aeroplane well out in the open. The Airfield Controller, probably Jimmy Jeffs, shouts at him over the loud speaker to come off the flying ground, but he takes no notice and clambers into the aeroplane, and falls out the other side, but scrambles back and starts the motor, with mechanics rushing at him from all sides. He taxies crazily clear of their clutches, and just as crazily takes off. Then ensues a most hair-raising exhibition of crazy flying, the 'spectator', of course, being the chief instructor in disguise . . . How many of the spectators this affair really took in I never could guess, but I expect quite a few, judging from the shrieks of horror and laughter.

The club puts up a wonderful tea with ices and sugary cakes for the members, competitors, officials and their aunts and uncles and all. Afterwards a few more exhibitions, the autogyro does its piece, the club glider gets towed up and sails around and lands on the mark after looking as though it would never come down, and soon those who cannot stay for the party are taking off and the crowd thins out, and pilots and staff peg down the aircraft staying the night and put the engine and cockpit covers on . . . [6]

The seven pilots who flew Spartans in the 1932 King's Cup air race (from left to right: Dudley, Louis Strange, McKenna, Adams, McEvoy, Andrews, Gibbons)

A welcome visitor to Hamble in 1931 was Robert Smith Barry, who had done little flying since leaving the RAF in 1919, also as a Lieutenant Colonel, advanced rank having been denied him not by lack of ability but by excess of independent spirit. He flew the Spartan with Louis, liked it, but nevertheless decided to buy a Puss Moth. His return to flying required him to begin a new and official log-book. He crossed through the printed declaration which said, 'I certify that the information on this and preceding pages is accurate to the best of my knowledge', and wrote instead: 'No. I don't certify anything. R Smith Barry, April 1931.'

On 27th June 1932 Louis Strange made a nostalgic return to Hendon to demonstrate the latest Spartan aircraft at that year's Society of British Aircraft Constructors (SBAC) show. The aeroplane was the first of the Spartan Cruisers, a low-winged monoplane with an all-metal fuselage, powered by three 120-hp Gipsy-3 engines. It had cabin accommodation for six passengers, who unfortunately had to climb in through a hatch in the roof. The plane derived from a wooden-framed Mailplane designed by Edgar Percival and built by Saunders Roe in 1931.

The appearance of the Cruiser at Hendon created a favourable impression. Louis was invited to fly HRH the Prince of Wales from

Sunningdale to Croydon in the machine on 22nd September, and two days later he flew the Lord Mayor of London and the Director of Civil Aviation from Heston to Maylands to open the Essex Air Display.

In October, with his wife amongst the passengers, he took the Cruiser on a sales tour through France, Austria, Germany, Yugoslavia, Greece and Italy. It was one of the rare occasions when he involved Marjorie in his flying. He gained orders for four aircraft from Yugoslavia. And had a lot of fun.

In February 1993 Louis Strange tested the Cruiser-2. Passengers now enjoyed the convenience of a door, and a cabin elegantly furnished by Rumbolds. Later would come the Cruiser-3, with a rounded fuselage and streamlined 'trousers' over its undercarriage.

Also in 1933 the company launched Spartan Air Lines Ltd, using the Cruisers for scheduled flights between Heston and Cowes, at £2 15s return for the summer season. Croydon would later become the London terminus. The Spartan timetable was rarely disrupted by bad weather. Even in the foulest conditions, pilots would follow the Spithead forts to the mainland, the beach to Lewes, then the railway north past Gatwick and through the gap in the Downs. Cyril Tubbs, an engineer and radio operator with Spartans after working for Supermarine on its Schneider Trophy-winning S-6s, remembers the dismay of Jimmy Jeffs, the Croydon controller when, with the airport closed to all traffic, Captain Robert Henry McIntosh would appear from the Isle of Wight out of apparently impenetrable fog. 'All-Weather-Mac' they called him. Cyril Tubbs also flew with Louis Strange on those occasions when the 'Colonel' stood in for one of the regular air-line pilots, and also when he flew home to Brooklands at weekends. Cyril remembers him as a man greatly loved by those who worked for him; modest and ever charming; meticulous in his flying, in his appearance, in his speech. 'The sort of man,' says Cyril, 'you would follow anywhere'. [7]

The full potential of the Spartans was never realised. Neither the heart nor the financial backing of the Saunders Roe team were in the Cruisers. Only fifteen were produced between 1932 and 1935, when Saunders Roe decided to concentrate its resources in the production of flying-boats. Although he had flown a Maurice Farman on floats as far back as 1916 and had piloted seaplane versions of the Spartan light aircraft, Louis Strange was no lover of water. Also in 1935 Spartan Air Lines was merged with Hillman's Airways and United Air Lines to form what would eventually become British Airways. Whilst he had been happy to play a leading role in the Spartan enterprises, Louis was less attracted to a directorship in a larger company such as Saunders Roe. He was not a boardroom man. Nor had his association with

Spartans been personally remunerative. He had gained little from his holdings in the company and had drawn only a modest salary for himself, most of which had been spent on his own private flying. He had found his personal reward in the air. But although he supplemented the family income from continued part-time farming on land he had bought at Fairoaks in Surrey, conveniently close to Brooklands airfield, he was aware that for his family the years in the aviation industry had been spartan indeed.

In late 1935, as the name of Spartan slid into aviation history, Louis Strange began to look for a new job.

CHAPTER EIGHT

The Spirit of Air Adventure

It was a preference for active flying, for the atmosphere of the aero clubs and the race meetings, and for the training of young pilots that led Louis Strange away from the boardrooms of the aviation industry in search of a job through which he could more directly encourage in others the 'spirit of air adventure'. In 1935 he joined forces with a kindred enthusiast: Whitney Straight.

Whitney Willard Straight was born an American citizen, of a wealthy industrial family. He came to England at the age of thirteen when his mother co-founded the radical education centre of Dartington Hall. He learnt to fly at sixteen and, as a student of philosophy at Cambridge, developed a taste for fast cars. He left Cambridge after one year to establish a 'stable' of racing-drivers and mechanics, and during the late 1920s and early 1930s became one of the leading drivers on the international tracks. He gave up racing in 1935 when he married Lady Daphne Finch-Hatton, and applied for British citizenship, granted in 1936. He then turned his considerable energies from racing-cars to civil aviation.

In 1935 he formed the Straight Corporation Ltd, under whose banner he would gather together several independent companies involved in the operation of airports, aero clubs, flying-schools and airlines. It was the beginning of a distinguished career in aviation that would bring him in the late 1940s to the posts of Deputy Chairman of British European Airways (BEA) and Managing Director of British Overseas Airways Corporation (BOAC). In 1935 he brought to civil aviation a refreshingly adventurous style and a keen business sense. Although he manned his London head office mostly with young businessmen, he recognised the need within senior management for someone who combined the continuing zest of youth with mature aviation experience. Who better than Louis Strange? He invited Louis to join him as one of three directors of Straight Corporation. The offer was accepted without hesitation.

For the next five years Louis Strange exercised his directorship not from behind a desk in the London offices, but at the company's airports and in the air. His log-book for those years shows him constantly on the move between his 'home' airfield at Heston and Straight Corporation's airports at Exeter, Ipswich, Weston-super-

Mare, Plymouth, Haldon, Clacton, Ramsgate, Swansea and Inverness. Nor was his flying restricted to commuting. He tested planes; he instructed others; he appeared at air displays and in occasional races; he toured Eastern Europe and Germany in a Vega Gull; he tried every new type of aircraft he could lay his hands on. He was in his element.

He was Whitney Straight's 'man at the sharp end', applying his inventiveness, his infectious enthusiasm and his own administrative skills to the practicalities of commercial flying. The notebooks that he carried with him on his inspections of the company's airfields show impressive attention to detail and overriding concern for flying safety.

Inevitably he was much involved in the corporation's training scheme. Anticipating a demand for pilots to crew the airlines of the future, and to provide a source of trained men from which the RAF could draw if necessary, Whitney Straight established Straight Aviation Training Ltd as a subsidiary of the corporation. It offered a range of eleven courses in piloting, navigation and ground engineering at five flying-schools throughout southern England. Straight's belief, shared with Louis Strange, that such training would play a part in Britain's belated expansion of military preparedness was realised in 1936 when the RAF began sending pilot applicants to civilian flying-schools for initial training before accepting them into the Service for further instruction. It was a reflection of the system that Louis Strange had gone through in 1914 before joining the Royal Flying Corps.

In his introduction on 'Learning to Fly' in the company's prospectus, Louis Strange returned to one of his favourite themes, inherited from those early years at Hendon:

> The outstanding fact about the art of piloting is that it is not dissimilar from horsemanship. The pilot feels that he is at one with the machine; that what he wills it to do it will do – not by transference from brain to the hand and the hand to the control – but by virtue of the fact that the aeroplane and the man are welded into one unit. This unity is the whole secret of successful pilotage . . . [1]

Although he usually moved with and often ahead of the times, Louis, born to the saddle, never would appreciate that there are many people, including prospective pilots, who have never been on horseback.

He was also much involved in the early administration of Western Airways when it was taken over by Straight Corporation in 1938, helping this to become one of the most successful airlines of the era. One of its several routes was the short hop between Weston-super-Mare and Cardiff, for which the return fare of 9s 6d (50p in today's money) was cheaper than the third-class rail-fare, and the journey far quicker. It became the first internal route to be flown at night, and was so favoured by week-ending Welsh miners that the entire fleet of de Havilland biplanes in their distinctive blue and grey livery and red-and-white-striped rudders was often called in for the last and usually boisterous service back to Cardiff on Sunday evenings. Over the Whitsun period of five days in 1939, 2,555 passengers were flown from Weston airport – a world record at the time.

Then there were the air shows and races that Louis helped to organise, partly to promote the corporation's airports, but in a wider sense to encourage participation in and understanding of flight. One of these was a Flying Flea cross-country race held at Ramsgate.

The mid-1930s had seen a burst of enthusiasm for ultra-light aeroplanes powered by two-cylinder engines of as little as 20 hp. There was a whole breed of these mini-craft buzzing about the sky, taking their generic name from Henri Mignet's Flying Flea. In spirit it was a return to the earliest days of powered flight, with machines often constructed and flown with more *élan* than skill. Of the Flying Flea cross-country race Louis Strange remarked:

> The spirit of air adventure was pretty much alive at Ramsgate that day, and I would not like to say whether the organisers, competitors or spectators got most thrills out of it. I know I was sleeping a lot more soundly the night after than the night before. [2]

Of course he tried the ultra-light planes himself:

> In one of these, of Czech design, built by Hillsons of Manchester powered by a 25 hp J A P engine, I flew from Manchester to Lympne, refuelling once at Northampton and only using a total of 8 gallons of petrol. On another occasion I flew from Exeter to Inverness in the day, averaging over 30 miles to the gallon, and coming back from Inverness to Ipswich I was able to average nearly 40 miles to the gallon. It was a glorious day, and with a pair of good field glasses I spent my time looking for hawks, which seemed to be very numerous, hovering at about two to three thousand feet. As soon as I got near one I invariably found that they were sitting in a really good upcurrent, and so I used these moments to gain height without using extra petrol. [2]

It was at the air shows which he promoted and in which he sometimes flew that he met a breed of men on whose services he would soon be calling: the professional parachutists. Early in the 1930s he had piloted one of the greatest of them – the Dane, John Tranum – for several parachute exhibitions. Later in the decade of the flying circuses he came to know the leading British jumpers: Harry Ward,

Bruce Williams and Bill Hire. They were to reunite in 1940 under very different circumstances.

Throughout Louis's time with Straight Corporation, he and Marjorie continued to farm, primarily for the love of it, and also to supplement his earnings from aviation. In 1936 he was forced to look for a new farm when the Air Ministry requisitioned his land at Fairoaks to build an airfield. He tells how he found a new home at Cherry Green, near Thaxted in Essex:

> I was flying over from Heston to Ipswich, and I saw a nice old farmhouse with lovely buildings round it, and a most tempting fifty-acre field right handy. I could not resist landing, just on the off-chance. A fine, upstanding figure of a man, a true son of the soil, politely asked me if I needed any help, but I just asked him if the farm was for sale, and he said he thought 'the Missus would likely sell it, but the price, like the land hereabouts, might be a bit too stiff'. Well, I thought I'd have a try, and I found the owner, Mrs Abbott, having tea, which she offered me. Before we had finished tea I had bought the farm, lock, stock and barrel, walk in and walk out; she paid the wages that week and I started paying them the next Monday morning.
>
> I went out and called in Ernie Bass and explained the position to him. He took it as though I was merely making a remark about the weather. He was foreman at Cherry Green, and his father and forefathers had been foreman there for over 200 years. He stood six foot four in his socks, and weighed sixteen stone; one of the finest type of all-round, genuine countryman and farming expert it has ever been my good fortune to know. His heart and soul were in the land. He never took more than one day a year off – to take the wife to Clacton for the day . . . [2]

Ernie Bass was to serve the Strange family well until 1942, when Government 'interference' would again force them from their land. It was perhaps indicative of a selfishness in domestic decision-making that Louis decided to buy Cherry Green without consulting Marjorie, who would in fact have to do most of the farming.

The publication by John Hamilton of Louis Strange's *Recollections of an Airman* had also been in part an attempt to improve family finances at a time in the early 1930s when they were particularly low. In fact, although it was well reviewed and has subsequently gained recognition as one of the classics of aviation literature, it brought only moderate reward. Recounting his family background, his early flying years, and his service during and immediately after the First World War, the book is a celebration of the spirit of the pioneers of powered flight. The factual detail – bumf, as Louis would have called it – is not always accurate, and the views expressed are distinctly individual, but the story is related with honesty, modest understatement, and with a humorous eye ever cocked at the ridiculous side of war as well as the dramatic. Though he lost his young brother, many friends and his own health in that war, there is no bitterness in his recollection of it. Nor on the other hand did he glorify it, nor seek to justify it. The realities and horrors of warfare are there, plainly stated. But rising above all, in this and throughout his unpublished writings, is the sheer exuberance of flight.

Louis Strange wrote the foreword to *Recollections* in 1932. It is a reflection of his views on civil aviation at that time:

> If these recollections help only to show the futility of war amongst nations my purpose is served. If this generation can achieve the restriction of aircraft for warlike purposes and confine their uses to adequate police work, it will have done well. This is a futile hope unless by means of extensive encouragement of civil flying, ordinary men and women of all classes can mingle on their week-end holidays with those of any other nations, at no more expense than they do now at their own seaside resorts. When that day comes, and it can come tomorrow if the will is there, war will be less difficult to avoid. [3]

This concept of aviation as a messenger of world-wide peace and understanding was shared by many at the time. It had become the vision of the man who had interviewed Louis Strange as a potential officer of the Royal Flying Corps in 1913 – Sefton Brancker. Before airship R101 carried him to his death on Beauvais Ridge in 1930, Sir Sefton, as Director of Civil Aviation, had campaigned strenuously for an extension of the Empire air routes and of civil flying as a contribution to national well-being and international accord.

For Louis Strange the fellowship of the air was more than an optimistic theory: it was a reality. He lived it in the flying clubs, at the international air races, during the dinners and reunions of aviation societies that he frequented, and during his many visits to Germany in the late 1920s and early 1930s when he met and befriended many of those against whom he had fought in the skies above the Western Front. He struck a particularly close friendship with Bolle and Von Leutzer, whose airfields he and his Wing had so effectively demolished in 1918. Now they re-fought their battles with hands swooping above glasses of wine in remembered tight turns and frantic side-slips.

This optimism and this belief in the potential of flight reflected the glow of aviation excitement that marked the early 1930s as the 'golden age' of flying. It was the age of the long-distance record-breakers, of

In the 1930s Louis re-established himself as one of the leading air-racers of the day

the airlines and the mail-planes reaching out across the world, of the air races, of the Schneider Trophy seaplanes roaring with untold power along the crowded beaches of southern England, of the air circuses with their stunt-fliers and their parachutists and their five-shilling joy-rides. Alan Cobham and Charles Lindbergh had flown into the headlines in the late 1920s, and now it was the turn of Amy Johnson, Jim Mollison, Jean Batten, Tom Campbell-Black, Amelia Earhart, Alec Henshaw and others to be promoted to film-star status by an enthusiastic Press. Although Louis Strange, like many others, considered the flying abilities, though not the undoubted courage of some of the record-breakers, to be much inflated, he appreciated the public attention that they directed towards aviation. If the aeroplane could eliminate geographical barriers, could it not eliminate political and social barriers too?

Apparently not. As the 1930s progressed, the prospects of peace through better world-wide communication or any other means diminished. As the mood changed, as Hitler's Germany began overt military development and Britain belatedly undertook its own re-armament programme, Louis Strange and others turned reluctantly from the promotion of flight as an active peacemaker to the more negative promotion of aviation as a military deterrent to war, and as an ultimate defence should deterrence fail. At the heart of his thinking still lay the concept of air adventure, although now expressed in more warlike terms, as in this extract from an article that he wrote in 1937, before Churchill made such stirring stuff his own:

> Unless the Royal Air Force is supplied with the best fighting aircraft in the world, and the best men, and sufficient of both, the peace of the world will be in grave danger. War will break out again, and we may have to suffer a sacrifice of life, homes and happiness, besides which that of the last Great War will pale into insignificance. Second only to that great trust, which we must keep with the Royal Air force, is that of fostering in the rising generation the love of the air and the spirit of air adventure in the same way that our forefathers fostered the spirit of sea adventure and love of the sea. We must see to it that encouragement is given to the youth of the nation to take to the air for sport and pleasure, as a profession and for the aid of industry, as a limitless method of modern transport, and as the greatest of all means of binding securely the British Commonwealth of Nations, on whose peace and prosperity depends the security of the whole world . . . [4]

At much the same time that Louis Strange was writing those lines, in Spain the planes of Hitler's Condor Legion were obliterating the Republican town of Guernica, ostensibly on behalf of General Franco, more realistically in a ruthless examination of the effects of mass bombing on civilian populations. Louis Strange felt a great sense of foreboding, and the gilt began to fade from aviation's golden age as Europe stumbled towards another war.

As deterrence failed, as appeasement failed, as Prime Minister Chamberlain's promise of 'peace in our time' failed, with great sadness but fierce patriotism Louis Strange, too old now to return to the Regular ranks, joined the Royal Air Force Volunteer Reserve (RAFVR). As a Pilot Officer.

CHAPTER NINE

Louis Strange Goes to War – Again

On Sunday 3rd September 1939 at 11.30 a.m., the Prime Minister, Mr Neville Chamberlain, told the country that we were at war with Germany. His words were well chosen and courageous, but his voice sounded sad, tired, disappointed. All his efforts for peace in our time had been without avail. [1]

Thus Louis Strange recalled the declaration of the Second World War. His recollection captures the sense of unreality and anxiety of those first few days of war:

My wife Marjorie and daughter Susan were on holiday in Switzerland at Glarus, and my son Brian and I were playing bachelors in our house at Highground. Three days before I had wired Marjorie to return at once, but so far we had heard nothing from them. We listened to our first air raid warning and the all clear, drove up to the RAF Club and saw all the ARP [Air Raid Precautions Wardens] in action or standing by ready for it. So many in semi-uniform and tin-hats looked strange, and the sky crowded with London's barrage balloons. Would Hitler's bombers strike at any moment now?

We had had rather a hectic night, for late on the previous afternoon a Green Line bus had stopped outside Highground and deposited eight children, aged from four to twelve. The very competent girl in charge of them would not wait for me to explain that I was alone in the house and would make a very poor nursemaid. We fed them and got them to bed somehow, and next day someone came and collected them and said it was all a mistake.

After some hours waiting at Victoria Station to hear if there was any chance of another train from Dover or Folkestone, and being repeatedly told that no more boats with civilian passengers were expected, we were just about to give up and go home. Suddenly we saw a train come in on No. 17 Platform, and the sight of hungry, tired, unshaven passengers told us this was another chance. Sure enough, Marjorie and Susan were among them, and were soon telling us of the sights, hardships and experiences of the five-day-and-night journey from Glarus. That night we watched the searchlights swing about the starlit sky, and discussed where we should start building the air raid shelter. Little did we think that it would be six years before all of us were together again . . . [1]

Within six weeks, Brian – who has been debarred through poor eyesight from Oxford University's Air Squadron and had joined the Officers' Training Corps (OTC) as a gunner instead – was in France with the 2nd Field Regiment, Royal Artillery. Susan also returned to France, to continue her studies at Caen University. She was not a girl to be put off by a few Germans.

At the declaration of war, Straight Corporation was immediately brought under Government contract to provide an air transport service and training support. Whitney Straight left to join 601 Auxiliary Squadron, and fellow director O E G Roberts joined his battalion of the Coldstream Guards. As the only other director with aircraft-operating experience, Louis Strange was screened from call-up until that contract might be completed, as were most of the company's ground and air crews. For three months Straight Corporation's transport resources were fully dedicated to the carriage of military passengers and goods in England and France, while its lighter aircraft were used for the training of aircrews and as targets for searchlights, anti-aircraft batteries and the Royal Observer Corps.

Louis Strange's main difficulty during this period was persuading the Government's Contracts Department to approve and the Treasury to part with enough money to pay the wages of fliers and groundcrew still on the Straight Corporation payroll. Problems of a more material nature, such as the runway at Exeter, he overcame with his usual directness . . .

With most of the east coast airports closed to civilian traffic, Straight Corporation and the other operators providing a similar support service, including British Airways, concentrated their resources at the West Country airfields still managed by Straight: Plymouth, Weston-super-Mare and Exeter. Also to Exeter, it was decided at twenty-four hours' notice, would move the Experimental Flight from Farnborough. When Professor Hill arrived unexpectedly to announce the imminent arrival of the Flight, Louis pointed out that the runways at Exeter were not long enough to take certain types of Farnborough's aircraft. Professor Hill, brother of Air Marshal Sir Roderick Hill, who as a more junior officer had served with Louis at Cranwell, shared Louis Strange's disregard for red tape. He immediately countersigned a hastily written contract for runway extension. With the hour a local firm was on the airfield, and by the end of the afternoon enough trees and hedges had been removed and sufficient ground flattened to add 400 yards to the length of the runways. The Farnborough aircraft flew in that evening. Three weeks later, when the Air Ministry Aerodrome Committee arrived to consider the possibility of extending the runways at Exeter, its feathers were much ruffled to find the job already done, without its authority.

The ruffling of officious feathers had never bothered Louis Strange. Of this particular episode, he wrote:

> During the next five years I discovered that there was a fine art in timing the method of not following the proper procedure, which heinous offence (in official eyes of Air rank and upwards) may have become vitally necessary to the job in hand. You had to make quite sure that you could get the job completed and results showing, beyond any question of doubt, before the said Air-ranking officers caught up with you, otherwise it was not worth the stripe or two it was likely to cost you. If you got the results, you did not mind losing the stripes . . . [1]

Louis Strange was to employ this philosophy on numerous occasions during those five years. He would get the results. And he would lose the stripes.

In 1939 there was only one RAF Squadron – No. 24 – tasked with providing transport and communication support for the Services. There was as yet no Transport Command. Nor did the RAF have any aircraft designed specifically for transport. The civil air lines and charter companies who filled this gap during the opening months of the war endeavoured to persuade the Air Ministry that they should be allowed to maintain their identities, their aircraft and their personnel, and so provide an 'Air Merchant Service', similar to the support provided to the nation by their seafaring colleagues. Louis Strange was a vigorous supporter of this concept. He saw particular value in retaining the corporate spirit as well as the operating expertise that had been built into the independent aviation companies. But this was to no avail. In December, the private companies and their assets were requisitioned, and their personnel conscripted, not all of them into uniforms or trades for which they were best suited.

Louis Strange was dismayed to see the company so needlessly dismembered. Straight Corporation was reduced to a small servicing and repair depot at Weston-super-Mare. It no longer needed Louis Strange. As a member of the Volunteer Reserve, he pressed for and eventually received his 'call-up'.

> On one grey, drizzling December afternoon, as I contemplated my third-class ticket which the Air Ministry had sent me, addressed to Acting Pilot Officer L A Strange on probation, and wondered how I was going to travel as instructed in civilian clothes yet arrive at RAF Kenley in uniform, it needed all my sense of humour to see the funny side of it. I managed a quick-change in a public convenience en route from Railway

station to RAF station. More than 25 years ago I flew a Henry Farman 80-hp biplane majestically from Upavon to join my squadron at Gosport (we'll pass over the two forced landings) and here I was in my old age having to walk to my second war! [1]

He had no idea what he was to do at Kenley. No doubt, he thought, some sort of 'holding' job until he could be posted to flying duties. He reported to the Adjutant, a boy half his age and twice his rank. His humour was no doubt tested further when he was told that there was no question of flying. He had been posted to Kenley on administrative duties. Some kind of assistant office-boy to the Station Adjutant, he gathered. Not bloody likely! Or, as he put it:

> like the gentleman's gentleman, I gave notice before I was dismissed, told the adjutant there must be some mistake, and wangled a 48-hour pass and railway voucher back to London forthwith. Next day at the Air Ministry I did not have a very easy passage: my particular flight plan was not readily accepted. [1]

His 'flight plan' was quite straightforward. It was, of course, to return to flying duties by the shortest and quickest possible route. The reason that it 'was not readily accepted' was equally simple: the age limit for General Duties (i.e. flying) for the RAFVR was thirty-two. Louis was forty-nine. For two months he maintained a constant attack on an entrenched Air Ministry represented by a series of selection boards. The answer was the same: too old. A year or two over the top they might have been able to accept, but forty-nine? Sorry . . .

Louis Strange draws a veil over the circumstances of his eventual breakthrough. He says that his persistence wore them down. More likely, one of his 'boys' from the First World War or Cranwell days and now risen to influential rank pulled anonymous strings. Even then, the final selection board before which he appeared did no more than pass the buck. They decided that Pilot Officer Strange would be transferred to General Duties if he could pass the requisite medical examination. They – and he – knew that he was unlikely to pass close physical scrutiny. Hadn't he retired from the Service because of ill health? And hadn't he only just risen from a sick-bed after a severe bout of sciatica? So instead of reporting personally for a full examination, Louis submitted the Air Ministry medical certificate that had been issued with his B Pilot's licence in 1928. It was accepted. Perhaps its passage through the corridors of the Air Ministry was again smoothed by friendly and senior words. Whatever the means, the outcome was that in April of 1940, Pilot Officer Louis Strange was posted to flying duties with No. 24 Squadron.

Where was he to report to? Why, where else should he resume his flying career but at Hendon, where it had begun in 1913 . . .

'Twenty-four', founded by his friend Lanoe Hawker in 1915 and now under Wing Commander Harry K Goode, was a happy Squadron, and its line-up of machines at Hendon did not look at all out of place in this home of ragtime flying. Most of the Squadron's aircraft had been requisitioned from civilian operators: DH Rapides and Dragons, DC-3s, Ensigns, Proctors and Italian Savoias stood alongside RAF Ansons and Tiger Moths. To fly them, there had been gathered together an equally mixed bunch of aviators. To a nucleus of Regular and youthful RAF fliers were added a couple of dozen Reservists, most of them with extensive experience of commercial flying. Pilots like Bill Ledlie, John Collins, George Marsh, Veasey, Gailland, and the Czechoslovakian aerobatic ace, Joe Hubachek. Louis Strange's old friend Earl B Fielden, who had flown for Imperial Airways and with the air circuses of the 1930s, was also there.

But before Louis Strange could lay his hands on that mouth-watering array of flying-machines, regulations required that he be tested. He had to be passed out as fit to fly a Tiger Moth. His embarrassed 'instructor' for this test was Pilot Officer Bisley. Amongst this young man's most treasured possessions was his father's certificate for his Royal Flying Corps 'wings', issued in 1917 and signed by the Assistant Commandant of the Central Flying School – Major Louis Strange. Young Bisley's embarrassment turned to relief when he found that his venerable 'pupil' thought it all quite hilarious, and was prepared to play the game with great good humour.

Louis Strange likened these first few weeks of flying with 24 Squadron to a school holiday. Like himself, many of the RAFVR pilots had held senior management positions in civilian aviation. To be relieved of all responsibilities other than remembering to salute boys half their age, obey orders and fly was great fun. The flying during those first weeks was throughout Britain and France in that entertaining variety of craft, and still without much thought of hazards other than weather, for the full blast of war had yet to fall on Western Europe.

Louis was able to fly a Proctor down to Netheravon to spend an evening with Smith Barry, who was also back in harness at CFS, and like his former 5 Squadron colleague, rather pleased to find that the harness now had a parachute attached to it. He wouldn't be staying at CFS for long. Smith Barry was, if anything, even more of a rebel against officiousness than Louis Strange. During the next two years he was to be shunted through a succession of posts by fuming senior officers until a job was found for him in India where, it was wrongly thought, his transgressions would be distant enough not to embarrass too many of his former pupils now elevated to high rank.

In early April, Louis Strange flew a DH Flamingo to Kirkwall to collect General Carlton De Wiatt VC, just landed after the evacuation of his force from central Norway. This reverse to British arms had come as a shock; the first of several about to fall upon Britain. The successful landings of British troops at Narvik and in the Trondheim area had encouraged the belief that Germany's invasion of Norway was about to be repulsed, but within four weeks the remnants of the British force that had gone ashore near Trondheim were in flight across the North Sea. Louis heard that Whitney Straight, in organising the operation and then the evacuation of a Fighter Squadron from a frozen lake, had been severely wounded, and awarded the Military Cross.

Then came the far greater shock of that spring. On 10th May Hitler unleashed his Panzer divisions into the Low Countries, then into France. General Guderian's radical concept of deep and rapid thrusts by independent armoured forces, supported by air strike and spearheaded where appropriate by the terrifying novelty of airborne assault, threw the more conventional Allied forces into confusion. The unexpected armoured drive into France through the supposedly impenetrable Ardennes added to the chaos. Holland capitulated within days. The vaunted Maginot line was outflanked. Other linear defences were pierced by the hard-hitting columns of tanks and motorised infantry. German dive-bombers and ground-attack aircraft hammered the reeling Allies, and shattered rearward lines of communication. The strategic withdrawal of the British Expedition-ary force through Belgium and France became a race for the coast.

All roads led to Dunkirk.

On 21st May an urgent call came for 24 Squadron to fly 600 tons of rations and anti-tank ammunition as close as they could get to Lille. John Collins and Earl B Fielden took an overladen Ensign into a field in the thick of the ground battle. After camouflaging the machine from marauding German planes for the rest of that day, they flew it back under cover of darkness with a precious load of senior officers who otherwise might not have lived to fight again. More supplies were sorely needed by the embattled troops, and the whole fleet of assorted 24 Squadron aircraft prepared to fly out from Hendon, via Croydon, to an airfield at Merville. Louis Strange was detailed to fly in with this 'convoy' with a party of airmen, there to act as Aerodrome Control Officer. He prepared for take-off from Hendon in a DC-3, formerly the property of the Dutch airline KLM. Half-way across the airfield, the port engine failed. The aircraft slewed to a halt just short of the boundary fence. Louis clambered out, and boarded a DH-Dragon piloted by Pilot Officer Bill Ledlie:

We left Croydon at 09.20 hours. It was a fine morning, the visibility was good, and to port, Old Father Thames was rolling peacefully in the sunlight down to a silvery sea, to starboard the Kentish countryside living well up to its reputation as the garden of England in all the glory of a fine spring morning. After the usual exchange of remarks about the met forecast and the somewhat changed appearance of Croydon during the last few months, we settled down to discuss how it was that Kent first started growing fruit. We decided that it was probably started by some Norman volunteer from Calvados at William the Conqueror's base hospitals after 1066, or perhaps the orchards were already there on the sites of Roman convalescence camps, to keep the doctor away.

However, we soon left all that behind, and began to keep a wary eye about us for enemy aircraft out across the Straits of Dover. All was peaceful and we made our landfall in France dead on track, and were sailing serenely along past St-Inglevert and on over the woods on the high ground beyond when just as we crossed the main road that runs from Boulogne to St-Omer our careful watch was rudely disturbed by some shattering cracks around us, and coloured tracer came up from below. Sure enough, down below we saw the once familiar grey-green uniform and the new-fangled swastika on the tops of the German tanks. Down among the treetops we were in an instant, and soon slipping in to land at Merville, out of all that trouble and into a great deal more, as the Messerschmitts and Heinkels clattered down at us from all angles, tracer and cannon shell screaming and thumping about our ears, setting an Ensign on fire and then a Savoia, and writing off a few more, while crews and control staff worked like slaves to unload the precious cargoes. The noise and thunder of battle and the change from a peaceful morning's flight to flaming war had been so sudden that we had hardly recovered from the shock of it before it ceased just as suddenly, as a squadron of Hurricanes tore into those Messerschmitts, and up they all went, whirling round, up and away, leaving only a few parachutes in the sky drifting slowly down in the sunlight, and the smoke of their burning aircraft floating away to the westward . . . [1]

Although the aerial combat had moved away from Merville, the ground battle seemed to be rumbling ever closer. Those aircraft that had not been destroyed by that instant onslaught were hastily unloaded and flown out again, with the intention of mounting a second convoy from Croydon. As soon as they had left, Louis Strange examined the Hawker Hurricanes that stood broken and forlorn about the airfield. When the Squadrons operating from Merville had been ordered to abandon the field in the face of the German advance, there had not been enough pilots to fly out all the aircraft. Some had been destroyed, others stripped of their guns and instrument panels, and the control-wires of the variable-pitch mechanisms cut. These were not beyond repair, thought Louis. His airmen should be able to patch up some of them. All they needed were pilots to fly them out . . .

Bill Ledlie had stayed behind when the other aircraft had left. he was loth to leave Louis and his men without some means of escape should the ground battle roll over Merville, as it loudly threatened to do. Louis persuaded him to go, taking with him a request for Hurricane spares and a senior fitter, and pilots to fly some of the fighters back to England. As the Dragon set its nose to the west, Louis Strange and his airmen went to work on the least damaged of the Hurricanes. The main problem was to provide some measure of pitch-control. This they did by setting the mechanism in fine pitch then attaching light telephone-wire to the control, so that after take-off a strong pull would put the propeller into coarse pitch. It couldn't be returned to fine pitch again, but by the time that problem arose the aircraft would hopefully be over an English airfield.

The first of the fighters was soon as ready as it would ever be. It was fuelled, and the engine was run. Just a pilot, it needed . . .

Louis Strange raised his head to the whine and rattle of renewed combat high above. The aerial battle had drifted back over Merville. Several Hurricanes and a larger number of Messerschmitt-109s were weaving their desperate patterns in the sky. Trailing black smoke, one of the English fighters lunged earthwards. There was a flash of white and the sudden blossoming of a parachute. The other planes were suddenly gone, leaving the sky empty but for the drifting 'chute. It was going to land on the airfield. Louis Strange walked out to greet the downed pilot.

'Would you like another Hurricane?' he said to the young flier who was gratefully shrugging off his parachute harness.

Within a few minutes, Pilot Officer Tony Linney was airborne again, heading west and keeping low. When the rest of No. 229 Squadron returned to Digby from the sortie, grieving the loss of 'young Linney' who they had last seen taking to the silk over France, there he was standing at the bar with a mug of beer and a broad grin. He would be forced to bale out again a week later, to be fished out of the sea off Dunkirk, and his own adventurous path would cross that of Louis Strange on two more occasions during the years to come.

As soon as the first Hurricane had been despatched, the airmen went to work on more of the aircraft, while Louis Strange scanned the western approaches for the return of 24 Squadron with more supplies and hopefully with pilots to recover the fighters. There was no sign of them. Instead came Heinkels, flying in low to bomb the village. The sound of ground fighting was also rumbling closer: too close for the officer commanding the Bren gun carriers that had been providing airfield protection. They were ordered to retire towards the north-west. The defence of the airfield was now in the unofficial hands of a Sergeant of the Durham Light Infantry. He had become detached from his unit during the fighting, had gathered around him a dozen scattered infantrymen, and was now operating independently. He rather liked what this apparently unperturbed RAF officer was about, and offered to protect the small band of airmen for as long as he was able. The offer was gratefully accepted.

By mid-afternoon the weather had become wet and stormy. The local roads were filling with refugees, moving in all directions, each telling the others that the Germans were right behind them, no matter from what direction they had come. From the chaos on the roadways appeared another downed pilot, trying to make his way towards the coast after being shot down to the east of the airfield. He was delighted to be offered a Hurricane to take the weight off his feet. Soon, the second of the semi-repaired fighters lifted into the sky.

Still no sign of 24 Squadron. An occasional brace of Messer-schmitts roared across the aerodrome or over the village on a ground-strafing run. There was the unmistakable crump of mortar-fire to the east, creeping closer. The Durham Sergeant sent one of his lads into the belfry of a nearby church, armed with binoculars, and from time to time went up to have a look himself. He was particularly concerned that the bombing might destroy the bridge that provided the only escape route across the River Lys to the north-west. He was, he told Louis, no great swimmer.

An incongruous Tiger Moth came hopping in over the hedge. Had he seen any stray Air Marshals, its pilot asked Louis? General Headquarters had lost a couple. Louis said that he hadn't, and suggested that the pilot might look towards the north-west, which seemed to be the general line of retreat from these unhealthy parts. The Moth hopped back over the hedge. Then suddenly, out of another whirling mêlée of fighters high above, a Hurricane swooped low across the field, to drop a message bag on the end of blue and yellow streamers. It fell 50 yards from where Louis was standing, still looking to the west for 24 Squadron. The message was addressed to him. It told him that neither 24 Squadron nor anybody else would be flying into Merville; that his airmen were to be attached to and retreat with the nearest British unit, and that he was to make his own way back to England as best he could.

The arrival of the message was timely. A few moments later the lookout came scurrying down from the belfry to say that Jerry was 500 yards down the road; ' 'undreds of the baskets!' he reported.

An officer on a motorbike – Lieutenant Soper – roared onto the field, and politely suggested that it was time to go. Louis Strange handed over command of the airmen to him. They and the Durham men clambered onto a petrol-wagon on which the Sergeant had mounted a pair of Lewis guns, and the strangely laden vehicle set off behind the motor cycle towards the bridge.

Louis Strange climbed into the most likely of the Hurricanes. 'Make his way back to England as best he could', the message had said. It was a pity about the other machines, he thought, after all the work his airmen had done on them. He pressed the starter button. As the engine warmed, he examined the controls. He had never flown a Hurricane before:

> I opened the engine up gradually to full throttle and boost. Making no mistakes with the knobs and taps, the Merlin engine took me off through the long wet grass, and in less distance than I expected we became airborne. Not wishing to become too noticeable I kept low, soon got the undercarriage and tail well up, took a good strong pull at the telephone-cable acting for the pitch-control, and heard the engine throb gently into top gear with much relief. All set for 'Home Sweet Home', just above the treetops over the Forêt de Nieppe, level with the church spire past Aire, with the air speed indicator creeping up around 300 mph. Some 200 mph faster than I had been accustomed to recently, but not a knot too fast for me just then. From the main road on the high ground just out of St-Omer a sudden clatter of machine gun and light AA shook me, and seeing tracer spitting down at me from the top of the hill on my left, without a thought of the consequences I pulled the control column back, and almost before I had time to think found myself at 8,000 feet. For a moment I was out of danger, and felt a thrill as I saw the coast ahead and the British fleet off Boulogne, but only for a moment, for I promptly flew slap into a perfect pattern of heavy AA, very noisy and very black and much too close. I got me down sideways out of this, but not before the keen eye of a Messerschmitt Staffel-leader had spotted me and dived to the attack. The shock of his first near miss was worse than either the light or heavy AA. I pulled the throttle right back, put the nose down a bit, and slipped in towards number 2 as he came. Numbers 3, 4, 5 and 6 all overshot me, and how I longed to have those Vickers working! But they were not, and I had to get down among the treetops as quickly as I could. Those Messerschmitts chased me up the village street and

April 18, 1959

Pilot Officer Louis Strange's celebrated 'Hurricane episode' was, like his tussle with the inverted Martinsyde, presented in popular style in *Top Spot* (*The Amalgamated Press Ltd*) (continued on next page)

down the château drive and almost through the château front door, until suddenly, twisting downstream in a wooded valley, I slipped clear over some sand-dunes and out to sea. The ships' AA opened up at the pack on my tail, and one salvo was enough to turn them back. The throttle stayed wide open till I was half-way across the Channel, still as near sea level as possible, and then I eased the control back a bit and had a look round me from about 5,000 feet. The black smoke of battle hung heavily over Boulogne, Calais and Dunkirk, and from the villages inland; a grim

The 'Hurricane episode' (continued from previous page)

picture in the misty red light of the setting sun, with dense black thunder clouds towering up further inland over France towards Germany. Red and black. It did not take much imagination to see the Nazi swastika hanging there in space with with such a background . . .

At last light I throttled back, lowered the undercarriage, and settled down to my approach and landing at Manston. I could not put my propeller into fine pitch, so would have to do it in one. It really was too easy . . . [1]

It had been a busy day. From the peacefulness of the skies above Kent into the flames and chaos of the land battle, and back again. How long, Louis Strange wondered, before that same chaos would be visited upon England?

His concern for the immediate future of his country was concentrated into a growing worry that he shared with Marjorie over the fate of their son. Brian had been in the forward British positions when Guderian's Panzers had struck. Nothing had been heard of him since. As the ragged survivors of the British force came back from the Dunkirk beaches and there was still no word, their worry deepened. Then came the dreaded telegram from the War Office. Their son was reported 'missing'. Two hours later the telephone rang. It was Brian. He was safe. He was calling from Wigan. Wigan, of all places! They laughed, and wept a little.

On the day after Brian's return from France – 3rd June – Louis flew across the Channel again, this time in the opposite direction. He

109

was to join the small advanced headquarters of 24 Squadron in Paris. The Squadron was now heavily engaged in flying passengers and freight into and throughout what remained of free France. Crews were at full stretch. Flying with No. 24 Squadron was no longer a holiday. They flew now in warlike skies, without arms or armour. From the principal air route between London and Paris, onward flights to the Front or to the base stores to the south-west were made by the Squadron's Rapides and Dragons. It was a time of confusion, desperation and wild rumour; of constant air attack and movement. And the movement was always in retreat. Le Bourget was bombed: 24 Squadron moved to Villacoublay. Villacoublay was bombed: they moved to Buc. The French Government left Paris: to be close to them for the transport of VIPs, the Squadron moved to Châteaudun. On that move, flying a Rapide out of Buc, Louis Strange could see the roads to the south jammed with refugees, vehicles of every description piled high with household goods. Petrol was scarce. Many vehicles were horse-drawn. He saw an Army lorry towing eight loaded cars like a train.

From Châteaudun the Rapides were used increasingly to fly fighter pilots to airfields where reserves of aircraft had been left, in a desperate attempt to get them back even further, away from the inexorable advance of the Germans. Sometimes they were too late. They would arrive at emptied airfields, smoke rising from the burnt hulks of the abandoned fighters. Louis Strange was reminded of the retreat from Mons in 1914. Except that this time it was further, and faster.

Soon they were operating out of Nantes. It was the end of the road. Orders came to evacuate to England as best they could. Louis later wrote:

> I remember how distressed the airmen were at each having to leave a good motor car filled with cigars and brandy – not loot, just goods saved from the Germans – and to pile them all up and set fire to them before we left. One airman just could not bear it, and drove his laden car off down to St-Nazaire. Somehow he got it on board a barge that was being towed back, and sure enough about three weeks later he drove the car, somewhat less laden, into Hendon. [1]

On 16th June, Louis flew the last of 24 Squadron's Rapides out of France. He tried to land at Caen to see if he could pick up his daughter Susan, but ground fire on the approach told him that the airfield was taken. He flew on to refuel at Jersey, thence to Hendon. When he telephoned Marjorie, he was relieved to hear that Susan had got away through Le Havre just before it fell to the Germans, highly indignant

Louis Strange, with wife Marjorie and daughter Susan, after receiving a bar to his Distinguished
Flying Cross – one of few to receive the award in both world wars

at being forced to leave Caen University just three weeks before she
was due to sit her degree finals, and bringing with her one of the last
Camembert cheeses to be evacuated from France.

The Hurricane flight out of Merville had brought Louis Strange a
bar to the Distinguished Flying Cross that he had won in his first
world war. The award was quickly promulgated and widely publicised. The British needed stirring news to lessen the impact of the
German assault on Western Europe and the looming threat that it
might not stop at the French coast. The evacuation from the Dunkirk
beaches had been glorified, and examples of individual bravery and
daring, such as that of Louis Strange, were given prominence. They
served the same purpose as Churchill's defiant speeches, at a time
when the Germans were staring at Britain across the Channel.

Amongst the written congratulations that Louis received was the
inevitable 'it all goes to show that there is a great deal of life left in the
old dog yet!' from a recovering Whitney Straight, [2] and 'this just shows
that the old men when put to it can do as well as the youngsters and I
take off my hat to you!' from Harold Balfour in the Air Ministry. [3]

Aviation journalist Bill Courtenay, who had written Amy Johnson, Jim Mollison and others to fame, yet who recognised far better
fliers when he met them, wrote: 'Dear Louis, I must send you a line of
hearty congratulation on the honour just conferred. It ought to

111

have been a Knighthood after your work for aviation these last 20 years . . .'[4]

But perhaps Louis was most touched by the letter from ex-Sergeant Lowrey, who added to his congratulations: 'you'll remember me as your Fitter at Abbeville when you won your MC for the Courtrai job, and on your first FE [FE-2b] that came to No. 6 Squadron . . .'[5].

For a hectic week after his flight from Nantes, Louis flew an Anson on several passenger and communication trips each day, snatching sleep when he could. At the end of that week, on 23rd June, he received a posting notice. He was to report immediately to Manchester's Ringway Airport, where a Parachute Training School was to be established.

Parachuting?

CHAPTER TEN

Parachuting Pioneer

When in 1936 during their autumn manoeuvres the Red Army dropped a full brigade of some 1,500 men by parachute, British military observers had been unimpressed by this first demonstration of large-scale airborne delivery. It was, they considered, a pretty stupid way to go to war. German observers thought otherwise. With the personal support of Hitler and under the direction of General Kurt Student, the architect of airborne philosopohy, an elite force of paratroopers had been forged. When Hitler unleashed his blitzkreig against the West in May 1940, the onslaught by fast-striking armoured columns was spearheaded by the dreaded Fallschirmjäger, the 'Hunters from the Sky'. A brilliantly conceived combination of *coup de main* and holding operations laid a carpet of intact bridges and softened defences along which the Panzers rolled into Belgium and Holland. This onslaught from the sky also struck deep into the very heart of military and political morale.

Amongst those who were much impressed by this airborne novelty was Winston Churchill, always an admirer of unconventional aggression in warfare. Even as the remnants of the British Expeditionary Force were reeling back across the beaches of Dunkirk, the Prime Minister was inviting the Joint Chiefs of Staff to prepare for the counter-offensive, including the use of airborne forces. On 22nd June he wrote a more precise memorandum to the Chiefs, in which he said, 'We ought to have a corps of at least 5,000 parachute troops.'

It was in immediate response to this directive that Louis Strange and six other pilots were posted from Hendon for 'parachuting duties'. They reported to Ringway on 24th June with no knowledge of what their role was to be in these parachuting duties, and with some misgivings, for they shared the aviator's traditional view that a parachute is a handy piece of kit if you have to use it, but otherwise should keep quietly to its primary role of cushion. What was the job all about? The Station Commander at Ringway, Wing Commander Blackford, was not able to enlighten them. All he knew of the matter, he said, was that it was top secret.

Flight Lieutenant O'Neill, as the senior of the puzzled pilots, went off to the Air Ministry to try to unwrap the secret. 'Parachute school? Sorry old boy. Never heard of such a thing,' was the only response from harassed staff officers much concerned with preparations to face the Luftwaffe now flexing its dark wings across the Channel.

Then on 27th June, Captain John Rock of the Royal Engineers arrived at Ringway, with some fifty soldiers – an advance party of troops, he explained, to be trained as parachutists. 'We know nothing about training parachutists,' admitted Louis Strange, whose initiative had by then promoted him to spokesman for the fliers.

'Neither do I,' said John Rock.

The following day Louis borrowed a Leopard Moth from Wing Commander Nigel Norman, at that time commanding an Army Co-Operation Wing at Ringway, and hurried to the Air Ministry via Hendon. He eventually managed to track down responsibility for the parachute training project to the Director of Combined Operations, whose Deputy (Air) was an old friend, Group Captain Bowman. From him, in an office in the Admiralty, Louis heard that a Squadron Leader Ross Shore had been appointed to command a unit to be known as the Central Landing School (CLS), to investigate the use of paratroops and glider-borne infantry, and to train them. Since he knew nothing about parachuting, Shore had gone to Henlow to make a jump – and was now in hospital with a broken leg.

'I'm desperately trying to get a replacement from Air Ministry, but the posting people say they haven't got anyone else,' explained the Group Captain. A sudden and sensible idea hit him. He beamed across the desk. 'Louis,' he said, 'get over to your tailor straight away and get him to put a thick stripe on either side of those thin ones. You can command the bloody place! I'll sort out the posting chaps afterwards.'

'Never were two stripes added to a VR's tunic more rapidly or less deserved. Nevertheless, I had to obey orders,' wrote Louis. [1]

The next day Squadron Leader Louis Strange flew to RAF Henlow, the home of the Parachute Development Unit where, with commendable foresight after the disastrously brief visit by Ross Shore, Flight Lieutenant Miles had already converted several training 'chutes for static-line use and had modified an experimental Whitley bomber for parachuting. Aft and lower-fuselage gun turrets had been removed from the aircraft to create a rear platform and a central aperture. From the platform, pupils would be launched by the simple but uncomfortable system of pulling their ripcords as they stood in the buffeting slip-stream, to be wrenched from their perch by the deploying canopy – a system previously practised from the lower wing of biplane bombers such as the Vickers Vimy and Virginia, and known as a 'pull-off'. For dropping through the aperture, the aircrew manually-operated 'chutes had been modified with a static-line system that would pull the ripcord automatically as the parachutist dropped away.

With the approval of the station commander, Louis Strange addressed Henlow's team of safety-equipment and fabric workers. He told them briefly of the requirement to train paratroopers, then called for volunteers to become Britain's first parachute jumping instructors. Ten came forward. 'Their names, which should never be lost to Air Force or Airborne history,' wrote Louis Strange who would thereafter hold these airman in the highest esteem, 'are as follows: Terry Oakes, Paddy Gavin, Bill Pacey, Kim Campbell, Lofty Humphries, Frankie Chambers, Taff Roberts, Bill Walton, Paddy Wicklow, Harry Harwood.' [1]

The following day they went to Bassingbourn to make the first live jumps 'through the hole'. Louis Strange reported:

> Aircraftsman Oakes was the first to go, and he landed on the Station fire tender . . . the remainder landed on or near the aerodrome . . . The next day, July 1st, with a few statichutes and some equipment, we all flew back to Ringway and were ready seriously to set about planning the training of the first British paratroops. [1]

That training was expected to commence within a month. It was a formidable task. Louis Strange and John Rock began with no previous knowledge of airborne training and procedures; supported only by such equipment and resources as could be rapidly converted to the role; and at a time when the War Office and the Air Ministry were much preoccupied with the defence of the realm against probable invasion. The division of responsibilities was quickly settled. Strange would be responsible for the parachute training; Rock (quickly promoted to Major in order for him not to be outranked by his RAF colleague) for the development of ground tactics and for equipping the paratroopers. 'Major Rock will inform OS8 if jockstraps and anklets are required', stated the minutes of a planning conference at Ringway on 19th July.

With little apparent support for this project, Louis Strange realised that there was only one way to get the job done. He threw away the rule book. If anyone asked him what he was doing and on whose authority, he would say, 'Can't tell you old chap . . . Top secret . . .', and get on with it. Without permission he had the four Whitleys that had been allocated to him flown to Armstrong Whitworth's for immediate modification of rear and 'dustbin' gun turrets into jumping platform and aperture. It was said that Whitleys with holes underneath were leaving the factory before he did. 'This officer,' complained a missive from the Air Ministry when it much later heard about this unauthorised modification, 'has no respect whatsoever for proper procedure.' To which Louis appended a note, 'I have if it proceeds.' [2]

With no time for further parachute trials, he obtained a stock of aircrew 'chutes and had them modified for static-line operation. He added twenty of John Rock's soldiers to the nucleus of RAF instructors, and brought in the stalwart Warrant Officer Bill Brereton from Henlow to lead them. Later he added the equally formidable Warrant Officer Joe Sunderland to head his team of parachute packers. He sought further professional expertise from amongst his former associates of the travelling air circuses of the pre-war years. Bruce Williams, already serving as an air gunner and just recovered from a ditching of his Defiant in the Channel, was the first of three circus jumpers to join him, shortly followed by Bill Hire and the greatest of the British 'birdmen', Harry Ward. Rebels all three. Men after Louis Strange's own heart.

He also needed a drop zone. Tatton Park, home of Lord Egerton and 5 miles from Ringway, would be ideal. However, the Army, other branches of the Air Force and the War Agricultural Committee were already after this useful tract of land. It so happened that Lord

Louis Strange (seated second from left) in typical spirited mood with some of his Ringway officers, including Earl B Fielden (seated on his left), Bruce Williams (squatting at front) and Jack Benham (seated second from right)

116

Egerton had been a pioneer aviator. He had flown his own aircraft from the Park as early as 1909, but had given up when his close friend the Honourable Charles Rolls had died at the 1910 flying meeting at Bournemouth, where the young Louis Strange had mounted guard with the Yeomanry. Louis Strange went to see Lord Egerton. When he left, Tatton Park was his . . .

On 13th July 1940 the first jumps were made onto the Park by the RAF instructors, dropping 'through the hole'. The embryo parachute training school was still top secret. 'So top secret,' said Louis, 'that the whole of Manchester turned out to see our first jumps.' It appeared that Western Command had told the local anti-aircraft defences, who had told the Observer Corps, who had told the Police, who had told the Home Guard, who had told . . .

Louis Strange was amongst the first to jump at Tatton. It was his first parachute descent. Other than a curt reference in his log-book, he leaves no mention of his several parachute jumps. It is likely that he didn't enjoy them. Leaving a sound aircraft in flight is not a practice that commends itself to pilots. Particularly 49-year-old pilots. But Louis Strange never led from behind. 'No, he never enjoyed his jumping,' said Harry Ward. 'But he never shirked it either. If anything ever went wrong, he was there next morning, number one in the first stick to jump.'

The following day the Army instructors jumped, all of them for the first time, making a pull-off descent as their introduction to the pleasures of parachuting. It was almost immediately decided that being hauled forcibly one at a time from the rear turret of a wallowing bomber was no way to go to war. The system was abandoned, and subsequent jumps from the Whitley were made through the hole.

On 21st July, less than a month after Louis Strange arrived at Ringway, the training of the School's first pupils, men of B and C Companies of No. 2 Commando, began. On the 25th it was halted when, under a streaming tangle of silken canopy and rigging lines, young Driver Evans crashed to his death less than 50 yards from where Louis Strange was standing in Tatton Park. He swiftly gathered together the combined expertise of the GQ and Irvin parachute companies, of Bruce Williams and of the Henlow safety equipment workers. They decided that the turbulent airflow beneath the aircraft fuselage had tangled the canopy and lines of the parachute, and that a better-regulated deployment system was needed. It was provided by stowing the same Irvin canopy in a new GQ back-pack which allowed the rigging lines to be deployed and fully extended before the canopy was pulled into the airflow. The ripcord was replaced by an integral static-line. 'Rigging-line first' deployment greatly reduced, but did not eliminate, the risk of major malfunction. This new parachute became the 'X-type' which with subsequent minor modifications would serve British paratroopers for more than twenty years.

A new aircraft would have been welcomed, too. The Whitley had a cramped fuselage, along which men had to shuffle on their backsides to reach the hole, the far side of which would sometimes smash them in the face as they dropped through it. The 'Whitley kiss' they called it. It was an awful machine for the job. Louis Strange tried to have it replaced by the DC-3, which had been designed for transport, with side door for quicker and safer jumping:

> In the very early days Group Captain Bowman persuaded the Director of Combined Operations, Sir Roger Keyes, to come to Ringway and hear and see our most urgent needs at first hand. I persuaded my friend Parmentier, chief pilot of KLM, who was second in the Mildenhall to Melbourne Air Race in 1934, to have a DC-3 at Ringway to demonstrate. After the demonstration Sir Roger asked one of the Army instructors which he preferred jumping from, the Whitley or the DC-3. Sergeant Dawes said, 'Well sir, the Whitley is like sitting blindfold on top of a sixty-foot well and pushing yourself down the hole, and the DC-3 . . . well, it's as easy as stepping out of the Tube at Picadilly.' Sir Roger promised to get DC-3s for us at all costs. He said he would get the Prime Minister to send someone to America, for I was able to show him a letter from Frank Courtney, one of Saunders Roe's test pilots, guaranteeing delivery of fifty second-hand DC-3s as the airlines were replacing them with later models. [1]

Despite paving the way, Louis Strange didn't get his DC-3s. Two years of jumping through the hole would pass before the Douglas Dakota became the workhorse for British as well as American airborne forces.

The concept of airborne delivery, as so effectively demonstrated by the Germans, involved the landing of troops by glider as well as by parachute. Parachuting kept Louis Strange fully occupied during his first weeks in command of the CLS, but on 8th August, two ancient Avro-504s that had once hauled joy-riders for Alan Cobham's flying circus arrived unannounced at Ringway. As their propellers jerked to a halt, Louis Strange was waiting on the tarmac for the pilots to explain themselves. He recognised one of them as Robert Fender, who he had known as a young test-flier at Farnborough in 1920. Louis didn't know why they were there. Neither did they.

'I can't tell you anything more than that we have had orders to come here and we're being followed, by road, by four gliders,' Fender explained. They had come from Christchurch, he added.

118

'What on earth have you been doing there?' asked Louis Strange.

'I'm very sorry but I'm not allowed to tell you.'

'Then you are all under arrest,' said Louis, and took them off to the Officers' Mess. [3]

Putting people under arrest so that they couldn't interfere while he sorted things out was standard Louis Strange procedure. He had an understanding with John Rock that when they received contrary instructions from their respective Services, one would place the other under arrest so that the least constructive of the orders could be ignored.

What Robert Fender and his colleagues, Peter Davies and Douglas Davie, had been doing at Christchurch, in utmost secrecy, had been preliminary trials with towed gliders. Now the trials were to become part of the CLS task. This Louis discovered when he spoke with the new arrivals' only contact, a Wing Commander 'Mungo' Buxton who, needless to say, was another of his old friends. Gliding! He was delighted. Soaring back to earth in a flying-machine appealed to him far more than leaping out of an aeroplane with a bundle of silk on his back. 'I used to find half an hour's gliding in one of Fender's sailplanes a great rest-cure,' he wrote. [1]

Another of the gliding pioneers at Ringway was Lawrence Wright who, in subsequently describing Louis Strange as 'already a legend in the service, his chest a patchwork quilt of ribbons', told how, when Louis had rejoined the RAF in 1940, 'the compilers of the Air Force List, unable to believe that Pilot Officer L A Strange could be the same person as the famous DSO, MC, DFC, sometime Lieutenant Colonel, had lately managed to include him twice over, and Louis boasted that for twelve months he had enjoyed two pay packets.' [2]

But his responsibility for the development of military gliding, begun by this handful of former civilian enthusiasts, was short-lived. On 5th October 1940, the CLS was renamed the Central Landing Establishment (CLE) and expanded into three sections: gliding, under Squadron Leader Tim Hervey (who as an airman in 1915 had been Louis Strange's fitter in France); technical development, under Wing Commander Buxton; and parachute training, under Louis Strange. Group Captain 'Stiffy' Harvey took overall command of CLE, with Wing Commander Nigel Norman as his deputy.

Relieved of much administrative and development work, Louis Strange was able to concentrate his energies on what now became officially known as the Parachute Training School (PTS). Basic ground-training progressions were evolved and practised on a variety of 'synthetic' apparatus, mostly devised by Bruce Williams. The length of 'sticks' of jumpers and the speed with which they could leave

119

the aircraft were gradually increased as drills were improved. Squadron Leader Jack Benham, as second-in-command, began to put a training manual together. John Rock busied himself with tactical procedures and the development of paratroop clothing and equipment. Early thought was given to making practice jumps from a captive balloon, eventually to be introduced as a training aid in 1941 and still used for the purpose today. Operational techniques for dropping by day and then by night were devised and practised by the Ringway crews under Flight Lieutenant Earl B Fielden, who as a circus flier used to drop Harry Ward under more peaceful and public circumstances. It was a time of trial and error, of adaptation and innovation, in which all played their part, encouraged and inspired by the example of Louis Strange himself. One of his less popular ideas was to equip the instructors with horses to ride up and down the line of paratroopers as they dropped, giving instructions through megaphones. Fortunately, he wasn't able to get the horses.

Progress by trial and error was not without its cost. The trials were dangerous, the errors sometimes fatal. Two more men died beneath streaming canopies before the end of 1940. There were no reserve parachutes as worn today.

Paratroopers trained by Louis Strange's Parachute Training School drop from converted Whitley bombers onto Salisbury Plain in 1941 (*Photo: No. 1 Parachute Training School*)

The problems were not all physical. Administrative obstacles arose from the continuing indifference of higher formations, and from the division in responsibility between Army and Royal Air Force. These problems would have been greater and perhaps insurmountable had Louis Strange taken any notice of the confusing and sometimes contrary directives that came from on high. Following one fatal accident, John Rock received a signal from the War Office ordering cessation of parachute training. Louis Strange received another from the Air Ministry ordering him to continue. He put Rock under arrest, and got on with the job.

On 3rd December, PTS was able to launch its first 'large-scale' parachute exercise – on Salisbury Plain. Louis flew the lead aircraft with Fielden. He wrote:

> General Montgomery had asked for paratroops to be placed at his disposal for this exercise, and PTS was able to supply them. A very successful surprise attack and landing was made and the paratroops, 32 officers and men, were landed safely from Whitleys by parachute with their equipment in a special container at exactly the right place and time. They immediately captured the Crown Prince Olaf of Norway's car (he had come as a spectator) to drive to their objective. [1]

Prince Olaf was so impressed that he treated the paratroopers to a round of beers when he was eventually reunited with his vehicle outside a pub in Shrewton.

It was time to prepare for Britain's first airborne operation. In fact, these had already begun on a very small scale. As early as August 1940, Louis Strange flew his first clandestine mission with Fielden into occupied Europe, to drop a Dutch naval officer, known as Mr X, near Leiden. There were to be many more brave Mr and Ms Xs of many nationalities as the training and despatching of agents became an important part of the PTS task.

By 1941, the School's first pupils of No. 2 Commando, now renamed 11 Special Air Service Battalion, were also ready and eager to go to war. In February, flying out of Malta in six Whitleys, forty men of the Battalion's X Troop parachuted at night into southern Italy to attack the Tragino Aquaduct. Although Operation 'Colossus' demonstrated a capability to strike deep into enemy territory, little material damage was caused and attempts to recover X Troop by submarine failed. All were captured. The Italian interpreter who had trained and jumped with them, Signor Pichi, a London waiter, was summarily executed. The Italians, frightened into the diversion of large numbers of troops to home defence, were more impressed by this raid than were the British War Office and Air Ministry, who continued to give scant regard and little support to the development of an airborne force. It was an attitude demonstrated at the subsequent court martial of Bruce Williams.

Bruce had flown as a despatcher on 'Colossus', and on his return had given his impressions to a reporter for the *News of the World*. Although one of the stated aims of the operation had been to announce to the world the existence of British paratroops, and although the raid had already been mentioned in the British Press, Bruce Williams was charged with unlawful disclosure of classified information. Harry Ward says of it:

> Bruce Williams did more than any man – other than Louis Strange himself – to set the training of Britain's paratroopers on the road . . . Louis Strange defended him desperately, not wishing to lose the most valuable man on his staff, but to no avail. Bruce had to go. 'You wouldn't think we were fighting a war!' fumed Louis. [4]

Bruce Williams subsequently trained as a pilot, flew Lysanders on special operations, and won the DFC. But he was a sad loss to the School at a critical time.

'By the end of the winter at Ringway,' recalls Harry Ward, 'we were in sore need of a boost. It arrived in a bowler hat and puffing a cigar on a wet and windy Manchester day in April 1941: Winston Churchill . . .' [4]

The Prime Minister's visit to Ringway on 26th April 1941 proved to be a turning-point in the history of Britain's airborne forces – and in the career of Louis Strange.

Churchill came to see for himself what progress had been made since he had called almost a year earlier for a force of at least 5,000 paratroopers. He found less than 400 drawn up on the parade-ground for his inspection. He watched others being trained in the hangar, then moved out to observe a mock airborne assault that would be made on the airfield – if the winds allowed. All morning, there had been gusts of up to 35 mph, well above the normal limit for parachuting. Churchill was aware of the problem, and as the wind threatened to remove his bowler hat, he turned to Louis Strange and told him that he was not to take any undue risks. Louis assured him that nobody would be hurt. None in the long-faced party shared his optimism. But despite the wind and a worsening forecast he had ordered the five Whitleys into the air, and had briefed Fielden that if the winds remained above limit he would signal him to drop the instructors but not the troops. He hadn't told anyone else, for it was likely that had he done so his order would have been countermanded by someone with more rank and less confidence in his men. As it was, the wind fell momentarily to a steady 25 mph. He signalled Fielden in the lead aircraft to drop the lot. Forty-four parachutists and a dozen containers tumbled from the formation of Whitleys to go skittering across the sky and angle into the ground. All forty-four men rose to their feet. In fact, one hundred and forty-four men rose to their feet, for Louis Strange had hidden a further hundred in the long grass. A mere forty-four assaulting the Air Traffic Control Tower would not have amounted to much, and there was just a chance that the spectators might believe the whole force had dropped.

Churchill said little. He was wondering where his 5,000 paratroopers were. As the party turned to leave the airfield, Harry Wood overheard Louis Strange say to Churchill, 'Listen, sir, you know nothing about this . . .' They walked off together, out of Harry's hearing, but with Louis at the Prime Minister's side, talking earnestly. His own record of that conversation is brief and pointed:

> I lost no time in explaining to him that even with the very limited staff and equipment, we could have trained ten times the number, had we had the troops available, and that I had repeatedly asked for greater numbers to be sent to the school. I knew what could be done, and I told him so, and of our difficulties, especially when disagreement and delay of decision between the Air Ministry and War Office affected our work at Ringway . . . [1]

Winston Churchill visiting Ringway in 1941, with Louis Strange on his right, and Wing Commander Sir Nigel Norman and Lieutenant Colonel John Rock on his left

Louis Strange, as always, punched straight from the shoulder. Group Captain Harvey, Nigel Norman, John Rock and others added their own similar if less outspoken messages, but it is likely that it was the straight talking of Louis Strange and the spirit of his instructors and of the troops who Churchill spoke to on that day that largely encouraged him to write to the Chiefs of Staff a few weeks later:

> I feel myself greatly to blame for allowing myself to be overborne by the resistances which were offered in respect of raising 5,000 paratroops. One can see how wrongly based these resistances were . . . A whole year has been lost, and I now invite the Chiefs of Staff to make proposals for trying, so far as is possible, to repair the misfortune.

The outcome of this swift kick in the pants was an immediate flurry of staff activity that would set in train the expansion of Britain's airborne forces to its eventual strength of two divisions, and a corresponding growth of the PTS. But by the time the new directive reached Ringway, Louis Strange was no longer there to implement it.

He had made few friends amongst the higher formations whose authority he had so often flouted, and although there were undoubtedly some who quietly applauded the manner in which he had overcome immense problems in order to get the job done, there were others who would be only too happy to see him on his way. The unrestrained manner in which he had laid the facts before Winston Churchill had no doubt embarrassed certain senior officers and Ministry departments. And no doubt they didn't like it.

Several months earlier Nigel Norman had foreseen the likely outcome of Louis's unorthodoxy, as Louis Strange himself recalled:

> He used to say to me, 'You'd better look out Louis, the job's going well, but I should hate to see the powers that be catch up on you before you've got it really well founded. Don't try to get away with too much at a time. You *will* go at it bald-headed. It attracts too much attention, and you'll find someone taking a pot at you one of these fine days.' How right he was. In the end his words turned out to be quite true. [1]

They came true on a morning two weeks after Churchill's visit, when Louis Strange was called into Group Captain Harvey's office to be told that he was posted, and was to hand over command of PTS to Jack Benham. Immediately.

Louis Strange never suggested who it was who might have 'taken a pot' at him. He went without complaint. He had the satisfaction of knowing that, in Nigel Norman's words, he had got PTS 'really well founded' before being given the push. He took no credit for this himself, but was lavish in his praise of the RAF and Army instructors who had supported him during those months of hard and dangerous pioneering. Only much later would recognition be given to Louis Strange for the part that he had played in laying firm foundations for the training of Britain's airborne forces, and for inspiring their expansion. Only a man with his qualities of leadership and his talent for walking through problems as though they didn't exist could have done it. Now that official support was more forthcoming, his brand of 'to-hell-with-the-consequences' administration was no longer required to see the job through. Proper procedures could be safely resumed.

Louis Strange was destined to return to airborne forces later in the war, but on 12th May he left Ringway quickly and quietly. Where did he go? He went straight from one hot seat into another. Literally.

Louis Strange and the Hurricats

His posting, Group Captain Harvey had explained to Louis, was 'for more important work of a highly experimental nature' where his 'initiative and drive would be made more use of'. [1]

That may have been said as salve to his feelings at being ejected from Ringway, but it would turn out to be true. He was to become Chief Flying Instructor at a new unit called MSFU, to be formed at Speke just outside Liverpool.

'What does MSFU stand for?' Louis had asked.

'Don't know,' came Group Captain Harvey's reply.

Nor did Group Captain Boughton-Paul, the Commanding Officer of Speke, know what the initials meant when Louis Strange reported to him on 12th May. It was, he explained, top secret. Louis borrowed the Commanding Officer's Tiger Moth and flew to London and the Air Ministry, where once again a top secret was explained to him. MSFU stood for the Merchant Ships Fighter Unit. His job would be to train Hurricane pilots and support teams for catapult-launched operations at sea . . .

When Hitler's plans to conquer Britain by direct assault had been thwarted, he had stepped up his endeavours to throttle the island into submission by cutting off her supplies of food, fuel and raw materials. The onslaught against Britain's merchant fleet was led by Admiral Dönitz's U-boats and surface raiders, but since August of 1940 they had been supplemented by the monstrous Focke Wulf FW-200C, a four-engined bomber with a range of over 2,000 miles and the appropriate name of Condor. By the beginning of March 1941 the Condors had destroyed 85 vessels, including 5 in one day on 9th February. The only effective counter to this menace would be a seaborne fighter. Aircraft-carriers were few, so in late 1940 it was proposed to equip a number of merchant ships with catapult-launched fighters. Because of its robustness and because the RAF had a ready supply of its earlier versions, the Hurricane was chosen for the seaborne role, and preliminary trials on a launching system were begun at Farnborough.

On 6th March 1941, Churchill directed: 'We must assume the

Battle of the Atlantic has begun . . . Extreme priority will be given to fitting out ships to catapult or otherwise launch fighter aircraft against bombers attacking our ships. Proposals should be made within a week.' [2]

The officer posted to Speke to implement yet another Churchillian directive was Squadron Leader Louis Strange.

Although the project was still in the experimental stage and MSFU existed only on paper, Louis Strange was told that the first aircraft and a team of pilot, fitter, rigger, armourer and flight-direction officer were to be ready on the 1st of June, little more than two weeks away.

By the time he left the Air Ministry that day he had obtained approval for the first crews to be trained on the experimental launching-rig at Farnborough, and for a Flight Sergeant and ten airmen to be posted there immediately as the nucleus of his staff. Then he hurried to Farnborough himself.

Leading the trials on the catapulting system at the Royal Aircraft Establishment (RAE) was Mr Charles Crowfoot, who greeted Louis with a wry smile and explained the technicalities of the scheme. The launching-platform was to be a more heavily powered adaptation of the catapults that had been flinging Royal Navy observation planes into the air from ships at sea for over twenty years. The apparatus comprised 80 feet of steel ramp, along which a trolley with aircraft attached would be blasted by a cluster of up to thirteen rockets, producing a speed of 75 mph and a G-force of 3.5. When the trolley was arrested at the end of the ramp the aircraft – theoretically – would be propelled into flight.

Louis Strange, never one to be impressed by theory alone, demanded an opportunity to put it to the test. Adaptation of the Hurricane to the catapult was not yet completed, but several successful launches of a Fairey Fulmar had been carried out. Louis had never flown the Fulmar, but didn't see that as a problem. Under the supervision of Mr Crowfoot he and the Fulmar were blasted into the air, flew a circuit or two, landed, and repeated the experience the following day. Satisfied that practice was more or less in accordance with theory, Louis Strange returned to Speke to set up his training unit, leaving the preparation of the first crews to the small team of technicians under Flight Sergeant Martin, supervised in turn by the redoubtable Mr Crowfoot, who emphasised his civilian status by wearing a bowler-hat throughout the launchings.

Back at Speke, Louis Strange found to his relief that Wing Commander Moulton-Barratt had been appointed to command MSFU, which would relieve him of administrative bumf and allow him, as Chief Flying Instructor, to concentrate on the training requirement.

There were operational procedures to be agreed with Admiralty representatives; a training syllabus to be written, not only for pilot training but for the preparation of all members of the team; the launching-platform to be installed at Speke; and the vast array of equipment needed for the venture to be procured. Louis Strange went about it in his usual way:

> In those days we really had to set about finding out for ourselves which shelf anything was on, from wing root bolts to spool fittings, TRD valves, and a hundred and one specialities which were not easily to be found at the Maintenance Units, let alone indented for. In a most unorthodox manner pilots were sent flying about all over the country to firms who made these things because we just had to have them, and at once. What did it matter though? As at Ringway we had a wonderful team, absolutely flat out on the job. Group Captain Boughton-Paul helped with all his might when we were able to follow the straight and narrow path of proper procedure, but turned a blind eye generously enough when we could not. Our jobs did not matter as long as *THE* job went on. [1]

It was 'to hell with the consequences' all over again.

Whenever Louis Strange did receive support 'from above' he was quick to applaud it. In particular he gave great credit to Group Captain Kirk and his staff from No. 9 Group Headquarters, who worked day and night to supervise the installation of the launching-platform at Speke, aided by Mr Blackwall of RAE Farnborough and Mr Sands of the Admiralty. Later, when the training was well advanced, he would credit Warrant Officer Lugg and his maintenance team with faultless operation of the equipment during several hundred launches.

Whilst the training facility was being prepared at Speke, the first merchant ships, freighters of some 9,000 tons, were being equipped for the role. They would be called Catapult Aircraft Merchant Ships (CAMS).

Modified Mark 1 Hurricanes with Merlin-3 engines began to arrive at Speke. Louis found time to fly one on most days, partly to familiarise himself with the aircraft, partly to clear his head of ground-level bumf. When he could, he flew down to Farnborough to see how the first batch of pupils was faring.

On the 31st of May, Flying Officer Davidson completed his training with a trial launch from CAM-ship *Empire Rainbow*. The first team was ready, and a further six pilots were well on the way to qualification. The deadline had been met. Louis was pleased, but not satisfied. He thought that ab-initio launches in the Fulmar complicated rather than eased the training process. Before making a decision he flew to Farnborough to have himself catapulted from the rig in a Hurricane. It confirmed his opinion that the Fulmar could be dispensed with. Thereafter all launches would be made in Hurricanes.

At last, everything was ready at Speke. It only remained to test the new launching-platform. Who should be the first? Louis Strange wrote:

> On July 7th I flew the first rocket-launched Hurricane off the platform, or perhaps in the initial stages, it would be correct to say that Sea Hurricane No. 7253, urged on by eleven rockets each containing thirty pounds of cordite, flew me off the platform and waited patiently in the correct attitude of flight for me to recover from the sudden start she had given me, and direct her on a quick circuit and down again. Anyway, bang went the first launch, and with it went all top secrecy for MSFU, also the protecting screen, which the blast of the rockets blew almost out of the aerodrome.' [1]

With his usual disrespect for bumf, he got the number of the aircraft wrong. He also makes a catapult launch appear easier than it was. It was mentally and physically a demanding experience, requiring the coolest of heads and the steadiest of hands. The

A Hurricane of the MSFU is blasted from the catapult rig at Speke

129

preparation for the launch and the exchange of signals between pilot and ground crew had to follow a meticulous drill. When the controller's red flag had been replaced by blue, and when the blue was rotated to signal that all was clear, the pilot would open the throttle wide, give it full boost, jam his skull back against the head-rest to absorb what could be a neck-wrenching jerk, force his right elbow into his hip to counter any inclination to haul back the stick as the aircraft shot forward, then give the 'OK' signal with his left hand. There would be a long three seconds while the controller made a final check that all was ready before tipping the switch. Then would come that explosive roar of the rockets not far beneath the pilot's backside, and a mighty punch between the shoulders as the plane was hurled along the ramp from 0 to 75 mph within 80 feet. The longitudinal instability of the Hurricane and its directional swing to the left had to be countered by holding one-third starboard rudder and one-third flap, and the tendency for the machine to sink as it left the platform barely above stalling speed had to be corrected with the most gentle of pressures on the stick.

Harry Ball-Wilson recalled his first launch: 'I could feel the G distorting my face, forcing the jowls of my cheeks back against the bone. Flash – and I was two hundred feet over the Mersey.' 'Flash Harry' they called him after that. [2]

Eventually the drills would become automatic and the sensations less remarkable. When pilots came to agree that it was a more alarming procedure to watch than to perform, Louis Strange would consider them trained.

As the training became established at Speke, Louis's days followed a busy pattern. The duty pilot would telephone him an hour before sunrise to give him the weather forecast. He would decide whether flying was on or off. If it was on, the duty pilot would warn all concerned, and Louis would rise at about 4 a.m. to cycle 3 miles to the airfield. The early start was no hardship to him. He wrote:

How often have I found, both in flying and farming, that the necessity of going to bed at sundown and getting up at sunrise is, contrary to general opinion, one of the greatest attractions of either occupation. Until you have found the necessity of being up with the lark and listened to her, followed by the great chorus of song which bursts into full volume as day breaks, you have never known the glory of a summer morning in England. [1]

Before breakfast he would supervise two or three launches. During the first two months of training at Speke he acted as control officer and pressed the switch for every practice launch except his own. If it was a new course, he would climb into the Hurricane himself to be blasted into the air before an awe-struck audience, fly his circuit, land, taxi back to the rig, climb from the cockpit, then turn to them and say, 'There – if an old boy like me can do it, it won't mean a thing to lads like you.' [2]

After breakfast he would spend no more than two hours in his office, then another two lecturing to the trainees on operational procedures at sea and in the air, on the characteristics of the Condor, on survival techniques, on aircraft maintenance at sea, on homing and interception. Then he would supervise the next batch of launchings before lunch. Afternoons would be filled by flying off to conferences; making arrangements for his mobile teams to load and offload the Sea Hurricanes, or Hurricats as they were popularly known, from their vessels in whichever port around the country they happened to be; escorting the constant flow of VIP visitors to this unique unit; flying on attack patterns with his pupils whenever he could, and if necessary, supervising more launches. And often there was a party in the Mess to round off the evening. Busy days – seven working days each week, for he took no rest at Speke. He seemed to thrive on it, exuding enthusiasm and good humour, encouraging, cajoling, leading. But the long hours that he worked and the physical demands that he placed upon his 50-year-old frame were soon to take their toll . . .

Louis Strange recognised the need for harmony within the teams that he prepared for sea, not only to handle the technicalities of an operation, but also to cope with enforced proximity in confined and uncomfortable conditions for weeks on end. As far as possible he allowed pilots and Flight Direction Officers (FDOs) to chose each other over a few jugs of ale in the Mess.

Louis also placed great emphasis on survival training. Operational launches would usually be made far into the Atlantic; too far out for the Hurricane to be able to reach land. When the pilot had completed his operation and his fuel he would have a choice: he could ditch, or he could jump. Ditching a Hurricane was complicated by the large ventral air-scoop which, if it scooped sea-water instead of air, was likely to pitch the fighter onto its back. For most pilots the alternative of a cold-blooded parachute jump was even more distasteful. Usually the sea-state would make the decision for them, and if it was half good enough, most preferred to stay with the plane. To given them the best chance of survival, Louis Strange provided ample training in dinghy drills and in basic parachute techniques. When he could, he would take his trainees across to Ringway to jump from a Whitley into Rostherne Mere under controlled conditions. He did everything possible for these young men, whose most formidable foe was not the Condor but the cold grey seas of the Atlantic, and when he sent them off to join their ships he did so with utmost respect for an outstanding level of courage.

They were indeed a formidable gathering of pilots. From the RAF they came as volunteers, and as such they came seeking novelty, excitement, challenge and, if they got that far, perhaps a trip ashore on the eastern seaboard of America. It was said of 'Stap-me' Stapleton that he came to escape creditors. The pilots of the Fleet Air Arm who flew Hurricats were ordered to do so by an Admiralty which saw nothing unusual in the prospect of its fliers finishing up in the sea. They were posted to the Fleet Air Arm's 'catafighting' Squadron – No. 804 – at Sydenham, Belfast, where initially they were instructed in launching procedures by their own training unit. Although not volunteers for the task, they were just as bold and spirited as their RAF colleagues. Altogether, Louis Strange commented, they were 'as tough a bunch of pilots to train as ever got into one Mess together'. [1]

One who arrived for training in July had a familiar face. 'Hello Sir! Fancy seeing you again!' The wide grin belonged to Flying Officer Tony Linney, the young pilot who had been shot from his Hurricane over Merville, to be bundled into another by Louis Strange before he himself flew out from under the noses of the Germans.

Louis was also well acquainted with one of the Royal Navy fliers, Lieutenant Bob Everett, known to him as a charter pilot in the 1930s and as a professional jockey who had won the 1929 Grand National on Gregalach at 100–1.

By the time Linney and Everett were trained, Flying Officer Davidson had returned from his first Atlantic convoy. He hadn't flown in anger during the crossings, but had been launched 200 miles from the Irish coast to return to Speke. This became common practice for pilots returning with an aircraft still on the ship. The first that Louis Strange would know of their return was the roar of a Hurricat dipping its wings over the aerodrome before joining the circuit and landing. If time allowed, there would be a few days of leave for the pilot and a little refresher training before his return to sea.

Then, in August, Bob Everett returned without his Hurricane. He had left it on the bed of the South Atlantic after killing MSFU's first Condor. Escorting a homeward-bound convoy from Sierra Leone, he had been coming to the end of his two-hour watch in the cockpit of his fighter 80 feet above the swaying deck of CAM-ship *Maplin*, when a Condor was reported 10 miles astern. He had been blasted into the air within minutes. The German bomber had fled. The Hurricat was only slightly faster than the Condor in level flight, and it had taken over thirty minutes for Everett to catch it. For the last five of those minutes he had been under fierce fire from the heavily armed bomber as he manoeuvred into an attacking position, but at last he had been able to empty his own guns into the Condor's flank. Dropping a wing and trailing black smoke, the big bird had plunged into the waves. Everett returned to the convoy. He contemplated baling out, but the relative comfort of the cockpit held him and he decided to ditch instead. Even though he tried to keep the plane nose-high, the air intake scooped a wave and flipped the aircraft onto its back. The Hurricane wasn't built to float. It sank like a brick. Everett had been some 30 feet down and still going when he managed to struggle free. He had been picked up by the destroyer *Wanderer*, and handed a welcome tot of rum. Ironically, Bob Everett was to die in early 1942 when, on a routine flight, his aeroplane developed engine trouble and pitched into the sea off Anglesey.

This was the first of several encounters between Hurricat and Condor, as well as with shorter-range German aircraft closer to land. Each operational launch was a daring adventure, which not all survived. No Hurricat pilots fell to the Condors, but the sea swallowed several. On the Russian convoys in particular, round the bitter North Cape to Murmansk, the chances of surviving a bale-out or ditching were slim. Pilots knew that before they launched. Eight of the Hurricane-manned CAM-ships would themselves be sunk by U-boat and mine.

After only four months as its Chief Flying Instructor, Louis Strange was posted from MSFU. During that time he had trained more than fifty pilots and their teams. As at Ringway he had established a unique training unit against all logistical odds, and had led it by example. And as at Ringway, once he had that unit on its feet, he was posted. Of his time at Speke, Louis wrote:

> The growing pains of these healthy young experimental units were many and grievous, but team-work and the ability to get round the regulations and procedure if you could not get over them won out in the end. As at Ringway, we all had a fine sense of humour at MSFU, and laughed our troubles off somehow, and had some wonderful parties when the long day's work was over. [1]

Those who knew Louis Strange at Speke recall him with immense respect. 'It was quite an experience serving under him,' says Alec Lumsden. 'He was, above all, human and kind, but quite dotty. He needed to be.' [3] Michael Lyne, who after flying as a Hurricat pilot, served with Louis as Flight Lieutenant Training, remembers him:

as a kindly chief and one particularly intent on not asking of a subordinate what he was not prepared to do himself . . . He never had the least aura of a senior disciplinarian, possibly because he wasn't good at submitting to formal discipline himself. [4]

The pilots trained by Louis Strange and those who came later were to give a good account of themselves. The value of the Hurricats was measured not by the four Condors they destroyed, but by the number of attacks they deterred. Once the fighters made their presence felt, the Condor force all but abandoned bombing attacks on shipping to work mainly in co-operation with U-boats. But even in this role they continued to be hampered by the seaborne fighters. By early 1942 the Condors would be largely driven from the North Atlantic by the presence of the Hurricats, to concentrate their efforts instead on the Gibraltar convoys. As the threat diminished and as small aircraft-carriers became available for convoy protection, the need for CAM-ships would pass, and on 15th July 1943, MSFU would be formally disbanded, having played a major part in turning the Battle of the Atlantic at a crucial time. Subsequent reunions of those audacious pilots would be delighted to welcome Louis Strange amongst them up to his last appearance in 1958.

Why was he posted from MSFU so soon? One story has it that he was sacked for having shot down one of our own barrage balloons that he thought was hovering too close to the circuit at Speke. The anecdote fits the man, but, alas, it is one of those apocryphal stories that attach themselves to outstanding men of action. The fact was that his Air Officer Commanding at Speke was Air Marshal McCloughry, who as a Major in the Australian Flying Corps had led No. 4 Squadron under Louis Strange in 1918, flying alongside him on some of the mass raids carried out by 80th Wing. With status now much reversed, McCloughry offered Louis the command of RAF Valley, with its four Squadrons of night-fighters defending Merseyside and the Western Approaches. It was a choice posting. Louis packed his bags.

CHAPTER TWELVE

Fighter Command

Before taking command of RAF Valley, Louis Strange was required to spend most of October at RAF Honiley to be trained in Night Fighter Control. But first there was a week of leave. It was the first leave he had taken, apart from an occasional day, for eighteen months. However, it was not to be a relaxing week. He joined Marjorie at Cherry Green at a time when a stick of bombs had just straddled the farm and, even more disastrous from his point of view, the War Agricultural Committee had ordered that another 70 acres of his pasture be put to the plough. In its nation-wide drive to increase Britain's cereal production, the committee had already converted 140 acres of his grassland to arable use. For a dedicated dairy farmer it was too much. Angered by what he saw as authoritarian vandalism, he decided to sell the farm.

He returned to duty unrested, and after only a few days at Honiley he collapsed in a state of complete physical and mental exhaustion.

Eighteen months of excessive work and inadequate rest – aggravated by sciatica, insomnia and the physical demands which parachute jumps and rocket launches made on his fifty-year-old frame – had caught up with him. So serious was his condition that doctors thought it unlikely that he would ever again be fit for active duty.

He spent three months in hospital, and was then ordered to convalesce for another nine. It seemed that his war was over. Marjorie had sold Cherry Green while Louis was in hospital, so they accepted an invitation from his old friend Smith Barry to stay in his country house at Conock, near Devizes. In fact the two old friends spent part of the time convalescing together, for Smith Barry, also returned to the RFVR in an experimental flying post, had recently flown a Blenheim into a tree whilst trying out a blind-landing aid. 'It didn't work . . .' he commented.

Springtime cheered Louis, as it does most men rooted in the land. He became impatient. Devizes was pleasantly peaceful, but the aircraft flying from Upavon and Netheravon, the crump of artillery from the firing-ranges on Salisbury Plain and the recently arrived American troops flocking into Devizes were reminders of a war that at last was swinging in favour of the Allies. Later in that summer of 1942 Louis and Marjorie moved to Warmwell in Dorset, where they lived in a caravan and took long walks along the cliffs, watching the convoys hugging the coast with Spitfire pairs patrolling above. A month of fresh air, exercise and farm produce put the finishing touches to Louis's recovery.

His appearance at the Air Ministry was greeted with some surprise. He hadn't been expected back. He insisted on a medical board, and persuaded the doctor who examined him that he was fit for duty again. He also persuaded his old friend Air Commodore Pike, Senior Administrative Officer of No. 11 Group, to have him posted to the Group Headquarters at RAF Uxbridge. It was a time of expansion – new squadrons, new aircraft, new airfields, and a new optimism as minds turned increasingly from defence to offence. Louis was given the job of working with the recently formed RAF Airfield Construction Companies to build new air strips in Kent and Sussex. He enjoyed the work, which required little time at desks.

On 18th December 1942 Louis Strange was posted as Station Commander to RAF Hawkinge. He was delighted. He had been bitterly disappointed to have lost the chance to command Valley, but this was an even better station: it was closer to the enemy. He also had fond memories of taking No. 12 Squadron to this pleasant airfield high above Folkestone to refuel their BE-2s before he led them across the Channel for their first tour of duty on the Western Front. It had been known as Barnhouse Flying Field then, with no more than a few Bessoneau canvas hangars and one shed built in 1912 by the Dutch flier, Megone, who Louis Strange had met at Hendon during his ragtime flying days. Now it was a front-line operational station, home of the Spitfires of No. 91 Squadron and the ungainly Walrus amphibians of No. 277 Air Sea Rescue Squadron. As Station Commander, Louis Strange also controlled ten smaller RAF units in the area, and had liaison responsibilities with a wide range of local military and civilian agencies.

Shrugging off the medical advice he had been given, Louis Strange – now in the rank of Wing Commander – moved straight into a sixteen-hour day, seven days a week. As ever, he relished the dawning of each day, and not once during his brief tenure of the station did he miss seeing off the dawn shipping patrol of 91 Squadron. 'That squadron could get into the air faster than any I have seen before or since,' he said, for he was much impressed by the efficiency and aggressive spirit of 91, under Wing Commander Demozey, and later Wing Commander Harris.

He was impressed too by the selfless life-saving exploits of Squadron Leader Spence's Air Sea Rescue Squadron. When he first

Louis Strange, Officer Commanding RAF Hawkinge

walked into the Squadron's crewroom he was again greeted with a familiar, 'Hello Sir – fancy seeing you here!' It was Tony Linney of Merville and the Hurricats once more, now promoted to Squadron Leader and flying Walruses, fishing other pilots out of the sea instead of leaping into it himself. Louis recalled one of 277 Squadron's operations:

> One day when a Polish Wing Commander was shot down just outside Boulogne harbour we had a terrific scramble to get him back. The Luftwaffe Air Sea Rescuers were smart but Squadron Leader Spence got to him first. Then a fighter squadron was sent up by the Germans to drive off 91 Squadron's protecting flight of Spitfires, whereupon the rest of '91' tore off to the rescue. Sector and Group were called in and the incident almost materialised into a pitch air battle, with all the available resources in the neighbourhood of both sides being called in. However, underneath all the fighters and from under the very mouths of the harbour guns, the Walrus picked up the pilot and brought him back, completing just one more of their finest pieces of work. My old friend Squadron Leader Linney was in his element at this work, and we often had the opportunity to talk over other times and devise new rescue methods. [1]

Survival of aircrew remained one of his major concerns. He remembered Ben, Lanoe Hawker and too many other friends lost in the air. The Hawkinge fighter crews, in addition to Sector defence, were much involved in fighter sweeps and photo reconnaissance deep into German-occupied territory. Losses were not excessive, but to improve the chances of escape for those who were brought down in enemy-held country, Louis Strange had his RAF Regiment Officer, Squadron Leader Palmer – who had won a Victoria Cross in the First World War – lecture the pilots on basic evasion techniques. He then organised an exercise to put those techniques into practice. At night, pilots were trucked into the Kentish countryside and dropped off in isolated pairs at various points some 10 miles from the airfield. Their task was to find their way back to base, avoiding the Home Guard patrols co-opted as 'enemy', then endeavour to infiltrate the aerodrome, whose perimeter was defended by the men of the RAF Regiment under the redoubtable Squadron Leader Palmer, VC. Louis Strange offered a bottle of champagne to the first pair 'home'. It was won by Pilot Officer Hartwell and Warrant Officer Waddington of No. 277 Squadron who, after finding their way to Hawkinge, persuaded two Land Army girls to part not only with their milk float but also with their hats and dungarees. In this dawn disguise they trundled past the sentries at the gate and drove to the Officers' Mess, first to deliver the eggs, then to claim their champagne, which they shared with Louis Strange for breakfast.

Louis Strange knew that his role as Station Commander was to support the Squadrons, not to involve himself in their operations. Indeed, he was expressly forbidden to fly on operational sorties. That he did not do so was not because of the Fighter Command order, but out of consideration for his Squadron Commanders. Nevertheless he 'borrowed' a Spitfire when he could and revelled in the perfection of its flight. Much of his travel to outstations and to Sector and Group Headquarters was by Tiger Moth, in which he would usually take one of his airmen, knowing how much the youngsters valued a flip.

Although he could not fly with the Squadrons, he found that there was much that he could do for them on the ground, particularly by improving their airfield. The drainage needed overhauling; the dispersal areas were inadequate and poorly served by catering facilities; and the runways were too short. In accordance with proper procedures he despatched proposals and demands via Sector to Group. He also sought to overcome the visibility problem imposed on Hawkinge by its 400-foot altitude above sea-level. Low cloud too often prevented flying from the airfield, whilst a few miles away lower ground would be clear. Louis Strange knew of several top secret airstrips on Romney Marsh: in his previous job he had helped to build them. Now he sought authority to use them as bad-weather strips for his fighters. Permission was refused. It also became obvious to him that the airfield improvements he had sought would be a long time coming. When another Spitfire ran its nose through a hedge off the end of an inadequate runway, he decided it was time to ditch the proper procedures and to improve his airfield in his own way.

He had already found a good friend in his local Army commander, Lieutenant General Stopforth, the Commander-in-Chief of 12th Corps. Louis had helped the General with temporary accommodation for troops at Hawkinge, and had provided aircraft to add realism to Army exercises. Now, in return, General Stopforth sent his Royal Engineers to exercise their skills on the airfield. Within a month the aerodrome had been properly drained, the dispersal area enlarged, and the runways lengthened – which also required the appropriation of a few acres of land. Several Army field kitchens were also diverted to RAF Hawkinge. The Sector's irate Chief Engineer wrote a letter reminding Louis Strange that as Station Commander he was only the tenant at Hawkinge, not the landlord, and that he had no right to initiate such major works services. Louis Strange ignored it.

His dislike of bumf, his accessibility, his enthusiasm, his reputation, and the work that he did on their behalf endeared Louis

Strange to all ranks under his command at Hawkinge. He in turn loved his Station:

> Altogether, Hawkinge was a station to be very proud of, living up to its reputation for hard work and hard play. It had the best Rugby team for its size anywhere about, and the number of visitors to its parties showed that hospitality was of the very best, and the Hawkinge dance band could not be bettered anywhere in the RAF. The WAAFs were a splendid lot under Section Officer Day. Her nickname was 'Happy' of course, and they lived up to it in everything they did. What a station! What a capacity for work! And how they enjoyed their play! Whether it was the Sergeants' dance, or a Squadron's sing-song, a 'scramble' and air-sea rescue, or overtime in the workshops, it all went with a swing, and nothing was too much or too little to be well and truly done. [1]

And then it all came to an end.

After only three months in command, without a word of forewarning or of explanation, Louis Strange received notice that he was posted with immediate effect to HQ No. 12 Group, as a supernumerary Squadron Leader. Not only posted – demoted. Not that rank had ever really concerned him, neither his own nor anyone else's. During his considerable fluctuations in rank he was once asked, 'What rank are you exactly?' 'Why? Does it matter?' was his response.

He demanded an explanation for this sudden posting. He wasn't given one. He didn't really need it. He knew why he was posted. He was posted because he had exceeded his authority. His contribution to the efficiency and safety of his Squadrons hadn't compensated for the bruising of official toes. He also knew who was responsible for his dismissal. Nevertheless, he submitted a formal request for an interview with the Commander-in-Chief of Fighter Command, Air Marshal Trafford Leigh Mallory. It was not immediately granted.

'I was so angry when my application for an interview to know the reason for my posting from Hawkinge was turned down that, to my shame, I quite forgot the war with Hitler, and started one with Command,' he said. [1]

When his persistence gained the interview with Leigh Mallory, it was left to others to record the outcome, for in his recollections and despite the anger that he felt at the time, Louis placed no blame for his dismissal. It was his friend Smith Barry who later told the story of how Louis, when told by the Commander-in-Chief that his big mistake at Hawkinge had been to ride rough-shod over acceptable procedures, had replied that his own big mistake had been made in 1918 when as a Lieutenant Colonel he had not sent a very junior Leigh Mallory back to his Regiment when he had been on the carpet before him for a serious lapse of duty. Smith Barry had himself been relieved of a command by Leigh Mallory, probably for much the same reason. He wrote of his own and Louis Strange's dismissals in letters to their mutual friend W A Ramsay, who had graduated from CFS under Louis in 1917. The letters, written from India in 1945, tell much about both men:

> Dear Ram . . . You're probably in command of something by now. If not, would you care to be Station Commander at Stapleford Tawney? I don't mind making it over to you. Leigh Mallory sacked me so quick – he never said why – that I never handed over and am therefore still Commander. But you may have it if you like dear fellow. It must be a nice little place in the summer . . .
>
> If you see Louis Strange give him my love and tell him I like his ugly son whom I meet out here occasionally. Yes, it was a pity Louis also got bounced by Leigh Mallory. You know of course that LS was worth 450 Leigh Mallorys, however much you may have liked his woman . . .
>
> Louis Strange – the bravest man in the world . . . [2]

Louis Strange's posting to HQ No. 12 Group at Watnall, near Nottingham, as a supernumerary officer was an admission that nobody knew what to do with him. The first officer he spoke with in the Mess warned him that the Air Officer Commanding (AOC) had no time for supernumerary officers cluttering his Headquarters, and that Louis would probably be on his way next morning. Shortly afterwards the AOC walked in. The Air Vice-Marshal's reaction on seeing Louis was immediate and instinctive. He came to attention and called, 'Good Morning, Sir!' before recovering his thoughts and his rank. The last time he had seen Louis Strange, 'Jock' Andrews had been a Pilot Officer, Louis a Wing Commander, back in 1918. Louis later commented:

> A great little man, Jock Andrews, and one who, because of his individuality and directness of purpose, was not destined to rise as high as he deserved. Anyway, I had fallen right on my feet. Jock Andrews just said, 'See if you can help Brian Thynne.' Again I was in luck. Group Captain Brian Thynne had been a Spartan owner in peacetime – he called his the *spitoon* – and I think he finally abandoned it in the middle of Africa, rather a long walk from anywhere. At No. 12 Group he was Ops Air 1, and suggested I chose a number for myself. So I made myself Ops Air 3c, and because there was no such number on the establishment everyone thought I was something special and left me severely alone. [1]

What in fact Jock Andrews did with Louis Strange was to make him a roving liaison officer within No. 12 Group, with the open-ended task of visiting the operational Squadrons, speaking with them informally, seeing what their problems were, helping as he could, and reporting back directly to Brian Thynne and the AOC himself.

The man and the job were ideally matched. It kept Louis away from desks and in the close company of the young fliers he so much admired. To them he brought the benefit of vast experience and the ability to cut through layers of red tape on their behalf. It also brought him ample opportunity to fly. One of five Groups within Fighter Command, No. 12 covered north-eastern Britain, with stations from Acklington in Northumberland to Coltishall in Norfolk. In addition to flying between stations in the Ansons, Oxfords, Proctors, Hornet Moths and the Vega Gull of the Group's Communications Flight, Louis Strange added the Mustang, Beaufighter, Mosquito and several other Spitfire types to the already impressive list of aircraft in his log-book. He enjoyed the task.

> I found I was doing as much as sixty and seventy hours' flying a month. I had no recognised job at all, I came and went as I pleased, no-one ever wanted to know where I had been or where I was going. I handed in reports once or twice a week about many things concerning the Squadrons' needs, and gave the Group as good a picture of the pilots' difficulties and point of view as I could, and the pilots as good a picture of the Group's problems. [1]

In addition to his routine reports, Louis was able to make practical contributions to the operational efficiency of the Fighter Squadrons, whose roles included day and night defence against intruders; shipping patrol; specialist sorties over Europe to hunt and destroy enemy aircraft flying at night; and, increasingly, short, medium and long-range attacks with bomb, cannon and rocket against ground targets in enemy-occupied territory. It was in this latter role in particular that Louis Strange was able to advise. The basic techniques of tactical strike had altered little since he had pioneered them almost thirty years before: only the weapons and the speed of delivering them had changed. Finding that low-level navigation and target acquisition presented major problems in ground attack, Louis went to Bomber Command's No. 2 Group to study their 'Landmarks' scheme. This involved the construction, from maps and photographs, of realistic landscape models of approach and target areas. Film would then be taken to simulate the run-in from landfall to target. It provided more than an aid to navigation: pilots who became mind-perfect in their attack route were able to fly it in poor visibility, thereby gaining surprise and cover for themselves. Louis Strange borrowed the idea from Bomber Command, organised teams of model-makers within

No. 12 Group, and introduced the scheme to the Fighter Squadrons.

He also applied his experience, particularly from his test-pilot and race-flying days, to teaching pilots how to get the best performance from their aircraft in situations where the balance between speed and fuel consumption was crucial to optimum radius of action.

And, as ever, he joined in the fun:

> Hardly a week passed when I did not find myself amongst a spirited and noisy crowd at a party and dance at Acklington, Catterick, Church Fenton, Digby, Wittering, Hucknall, Coltishall . . . Never in my life, I think, either before or since, did I make so many good friends, have such a very good time, and meet so many very gallant air crews as those in No. 12 Group. [1]

One who remembers Louis Strange having 'a very good time' is aviation historian and writer Richard Thownshend Bickers:

> I met him at Watnall in 1942. He was very popular and admired, and to me, meeting him was like touching a bare 220-volt wire. He exuded exuberant energy and a strong, attractive personality. I recall the weekly all-ranks dance in the NAAFI, seeing LS dashing around the floor with a variety of attractive WAAF, all of whom obviously enjoyed partnering him despite the disparity in years . . .
>
> Louis Strange was one of the most electrifying personalities I ever met; only Douglas Bader made the same instant forceful impact. [3]

In late 1943, Air Marshal Sir Roderick Hill took over from Leigh Mallory as Commander-in-Chief Fighter Command. Louis Strange had served with Sir Roderick at Cranwell in 1920, and in December was summoned to see him at his Bentley Priory headquarters. It was for more than reminiscence. Sir Roderick was one who knew the value of Louis Strange. Within a week Louis was a Wing Commander once more, posted to HQ 46 Group in support of Britain's airborne forces.

CHAPTER THIRTEEN

Airborne Forces

After Churchill's visit to Ringway in 1941, the development of British airborne forces had quickly gathered pace. The Parachute Training School founded by Louis Strange had at last been given the backing that he had fought for, and had been enlarged to provide the troops for the 1st Parachute Brigade, a force that within the next two years would grow to two Divisions. Early in 1942 Major John Frost and 120 men demonstrated the effectiveness of the force with a night parachute raid against a German radar installation on the French cliffs at Bruneval. Later that year men of the 1st Brigade took part in the Allied invasion of North Africa where, although mis-employed as paratroopers, they fought with great distinction to earn their name of 'Red Devils' from an impressed foe. They gained further battle honours in Sicily in 1943, despite wildly inaccurate delivery by the United States Army Air Force (USAAF) Troop Carrier Command. By the end of the year, the 1st and 6th British Airborne Divisions were being prepared for the invasion of mainland Europe. To deliver and support these forces, the RAF was now dedicating two specialist transport Groups: No. 38, already formed from No. 38 Wing of early Ringway days, and a new Group, No. 46. It was to No. 46 Group as Wing Commander Operations that Louis Strange was posted.

As one of the first three staff officers appointed to the Group, which was so far without a Headquarters of its own, Louis Strange was immediately attached to HQ No. 38 Group at Netheravon, where he arrived on 27th December 1943. He found himself amongst friends, fellow pioneers of airborne forces from Ringway. There were paratroop officers Martin Lindsay and Bill Bradish; Parachute Jumping Instructors Harry Ward and Bill Hire; glider pilots Robert Fender and Lawrence Wright; fliers Earl B Fielden and 'Mac' McMonies. Sadly, others were missing. Jack Benham and Nigel Norman had died in aircraft crashes, John Rock in a glider.

To his delight, Louis found that his AOC was to be – yet again – an officer who had served under his own command during the First World War, 'Fido' Fiddament, now an Air Commodore.

Louis Strange's job as the first Ops officer of the new formation was to learn what he could from the staffs and stations of No. 38 Group, transpose it into a training programme and operational procedures for 46, and pass these for immediate action to the new Dakota squadrons now forming on recently constructed airfields at Down Ampney, Broadwell and Blakehill Farm. He also began to beg, borrow and steal as many of 38 Group's staff and as much of its equipment as he could without making too much of a nuisance of himself. For once he received heartening co-operation, particularly from within 38 Group under its energetic commander Air Vice-Marshal 'Holly' Hollingsworth. Everyone knew that time was short for the new Group to ready itself for the anticipated events of that summer. Everyone was pulling and pushing 46 Group in the same direction: towards the invasion of 'Fortress Europe'. Everyone, that was, except Air-Chief Marshal Leigh Mallory who, as Eisenhower's Air Commander, forecast 80% casualties to airborne forces and advised against their use at all. Eisenhower as Allied Supreme Commander and his immediate deputy, Air-Chief Marshal Tedder, overruled Leigh Mallory, no doubt to the delight of Louis Strange, amongst others.

In the preparation of the new Group, the key problem was the training of crews mostly new to transport support, some of them new to the Dakota itself. Louis arranged to attach his first crews to 38 Group stations to learn parachute-dropping and glider-towing pro-

By 1944, when Louis Strange returned to work with Airborne Forces, the Douglas Dakota (background) that he had recommended three years earlier had at last replaced the Whitley as the major paratrooping vehicle (*Photo: No. 1 Parachute Training School*)

cedures. Then, as he had done in the First World War, he used these 'trained' crews to instruct others within their own Squadrons.

On 23rd February he flew as co-pilot to Flight Lieutenant Mountford on the first live parachute drop by aircraft of No. 46 Group. From that day until mid-April hardly a day passed without paratroop-dropping and glider-towing practices. And hardly a day passed without Louis Strange appearing somewhere on Salisbury Plain at first light to observe the dawn drops – to savour the lark-song and the colours of sunrise; the safe blossoming and gentle drift of parachutes in the sky; the chatter of young paratroopers clustered round the NAAFI wagon at the side of the drop zone; the chorus of 'Rock-a-bye baby, in the tree top', which they sang to one of their number dangling from a tall tree into which a wayward wind had drifted him.

He enjoyed piloting a Dakota on some of the practice sorties, and took pleasure in the many flights in an Auster or a Proctor between the numerous units and stations on his visiting lists, flying above the countryside over which he had puttered in 1914 in a Henry Farman. Tony Dudgeon, at that time Officer Commanding Flying at RAF Down Ampney, remembers one of those flights. He was an officer of similar spirit to Louis Strange. In the heroic defence of RAF Habbaniyah against heavy Iraqi ground forces in 1941, he had quite unofficially converted twenty-seven Oxford training planes into bombers, and had flown one himself in the successful actions that saved the base. Now he was occupying the right-hand seat of a Proctor being flown back to Netheravon by Louis, beneath a cloud base that forced them down into one of the narrowing valleys leading towards the completely obscured airfield.

'Look out for Friesians on your side,' said Louis.

'Friesian what?' asked Tony Dudgeon.

'Friesian cows. Tell me when you see them.'

'Right,' A few moments later he reported Friesians off the starboard wing.

Louis took a quick glance. 'They're Herefords, you bloody fool. Friesians are black-and-white jobs.'

'Right,' said Tony Dudgeon, and a few moments later yelled, 'There they are!'

Louis Strange immediately hauled back the stick, lifted the Proctor straight up into the base of the cloud, and a few moments later put it down in almost zero visibility on Netheravon airfield.

'Do you always navigate by cows?' asked Tony Dudgeon as they climbed from the cockpit.

'Not at milking time,' came the reply. [1]

With only four or perhaps five months in which to prepare for a massive airborne assault, probably by night, the problems that confronted Louis Strange as he toured his stations were considerable. Gradually they were resolved through intensive and demanding training, which was put into effect in a series of progressively larger rehearsals, culminating in a mass drop by 150 aircraft on 14th April on drop zones close to Shrewton, where in 1940 Louis Strange had mounted the first British airborne exercise with his five old Whitleys. By the 1st of June, No. 46 Group was ready to play its part in the greatest seaborne and airborne invasion of all time.

Air Commodore Fiddament, as AOC of the Group, was in no doubt where the credit lay for having won this race against time. When the D-Day dust had settled he would write:

> Dear Louis, I have been intending to write to you ever since D-Day to thank you for all the sterling work you did for 46 Group in the Airborne Training. All of us here know quite well that, but for you, the Group would not have been ready on the day. I realise . . . the difficulties you had to contend with – not the least of which arose from the set-up of the two Groups and some of the personalities involved. How well you succeeded in overcoming even those difficulties was proved by the glowing tributes paid to you by both Holly and Bladin when I was at Netheravon recently . . . I am deeply grateful to you . . .

He ended the letter with a fine compliment addressed by an Air Commodore to an acting Wing Commander: 'I would again serve under you, most willingly.' [2]

By June, beneath an umbrella of almost total air superiority, the harbours and creeks of southern England were crammed with an invasion fleet of some 5,000 vessels. Orderly ranks of gliders and transport aircraft covered its airfields. Tanks, artillery, strange amphibious machines called 'Ducks' (actually DUKWS), and support vehicles of every kind lined its roads and hid beneath its trees. Depots bulged with fuel, food, munitions and the full ordnance of battle. It was said that beneath such a weight of military hardware, only the barrage balloons kept England afloat.

All was ready. But few knew where they were going, or when. Security was vital. As Allied Supreme Commander, General Dwight D Eisenhower knew that if the Germans had as little as forty-eight hours' warning of where the blow would fall, his chances of gaining a foothold on the French coast would be slim. Common sense suggested that he would take the shortest route across the Channel into the Pas de Calais, and Eisenhower reinforced common sense with well contrived deception. That was where the Germans expected him . . .

On the 1st of June the briefings for Operation 'Overlord' began. Within encampments and headquarters sealed from contact with the outside world, in rooms with covered windows and a sentry at each door, first the commanders, then their staffs, then as many of their men as needed to know were told of the part they were to play on D-Day. It was not to the Pas de Calais but to the beaches and drop zones of Normandy that they were bound. Five Divisions under General Bernard Montgomery would go ashore at dawn on 5th June: the 1st US Army on Utah and Omaha beaches on the right, the British 2nd Army on Gold, Juno and Sword beaches on the left. Before then, three airborne divisions would be dropped in darkness to protect the flanks: the American 82nd and 101st on the right, the British 6th on the left. It was planned to put 156,000 fighting men into Normandy during the first and critical twenty-four hours. Their task would be to establish a beach-head some 10 miles in depth, then hold it against counter-attack whilst massive reinforcement was poured in.

The intense seriousness of the briefings was not without its lighter moments. Louis Strange, with some prior knowledge of the invasion plans, had early booked his place on the lead aircraft of the airborne assault, quite contrary to orders that forebade staff officers from any active participation in D-Day. Fortunately, because he was attached to 38 Group and had his own 46 Group Headquarters in London, nobody really ever knew what Louis Strange was doing. When he attended the detailed briefing for Group staffs, he found on the scale model that awaited them that his drop-zone between the rivers Orne and Dives was covered by what appeared to be an industrial estate. He turned to remonstrate with the briefing officer, who replied blandly 'What buildings?' When Louis turned back to the board, the industrial estate had disappeared – swiftly replaced on the outskirts of Caen from which Lawrence Wright had previously moved it. 'Must be seeing things, Louis,' he suggested. [3]

Bad weather delayed 'Overlord' by one anxious day. In some of his most graphic writing, Louis Strange tells of those twenty-four hours and of the events that followed:

At Zero minus 24 hours the wheels of the great machine began to turn. Gliders were being formed up at the end of runways, tow-ropes laid out. Aircraft were formed up, each on the exact spot allotted to it. Crews, equipment, and each respective loading list checked, examined and numbered. The loading of equipment started. By Zero minus 12 hours every piece was in place, and on a hundred airfields over the Midlands and southern England thousands of aircraft and gliders were in their exact positions ready for the take-off.

148

Zero minus 4 hours, and the troops are beginning to arrive in lorry loads from their transit camps. Each team checks its aircraft and equipment, gets to know the aircrew, fits its parachutes. Then they depart to the canteen, improvised in one of the hangars, for a final meal.

Zero minus 1 hour. They now gather round their aircraft again, helping each other on with their parachutes, each adjusting his own special weapons in their proper place. They blacken each others' faces and tie on camouflage netting. Their commanding officer comes round and has a final chat with each group.

Zero minus 30 minutes. A hunting horn is heard . . . the order to emplane goes round. They clamber aboard, black grinning faces in the doorway of the Dakota in the half light. A thousand wisecracks from a thousand aircraft in those few moments.

Fifteen minutes to go, and the aircrews climb on board. Pilots and navigators have just come from a final 'met' briefing, last minute adjustments to flight plans have been made. The flight engineer takes off the control locking devices, and holds them up for the pilot to see. He is the last to climb in and haul the steps up after him. The pilot watches the second-hand of his watch, synchronised with thousands of others: it ticks round to start-engine time, six minutes before take off. He checks 'all correct' over the intercom to each member of the crew. Five minutes to go and he presses the starter button; the port airscrew turns slowly, then flicks over into a low throttle roar. The starboard engine follows suit. All round the perimeter track aircraft after aircraft springs to life, and quivers and shifts a little on the brakes as the pilot tests each engine to full throttle . . .

And thus, at 23.15 hours on June 5th 1944, Squadron Leader 'Dusty' Miller, the pilot of the first aircraft of the leading squadron of 46 Group, in which I was acting as Group observer, assistant despatcher, general cabin-boy and steward to the paratroopers, eased off the brakes and moved the throttles forward. The aircraft rolled, taxi-ing and turning onto the end of the runway, gathered speed and took off into the west, where the last red glow of the sun lingered.

The night was clear, and from the astrodome there was still light enough to see the streams of Dakotas in arrowhead threes following us up from the runway. Every aircraft of the squadron got away like clockwork, and we settled onto the first leg of our course. The flight plan for such a vast number of aircraft and gliders was a complicated work of art. They were converging on a very concentrated area over which each must appear at its own precise time. There could be no question of any one airfield's quota not being in proper station when entering the stream on the way over.

After a leg NNE, another South and a third WSW in order to conform

149

to the flight plan, the fourth took us from a point near Basingstoke to the coast at Littlehampton. I could clearly see Arundel Castle from 1500 feet. The first thing I noticed as we got well out over the Channel was what at first appeared to be a rough sea, with many white horses ahead. On passing over and looking down I saw that these were the bow-waves of hundreds of sea-going craft of every description, all in perfect order and formation. The moment gave us the greatest thrill. The hunt was up! We of airborne forces had started from scratch, but we were now overhauling the main body to lead the vanguard in to the kill. It was a good thirty minutes before we passed the leading assault craft, and all that time the sea below was a mass of ships and vessels surging along, the like of which had never been seen before, and which gave an impression of irresistible might.

Whilst still a long way off we saw the great flashes of the 100-Lancaster bomber raid on the battery of coastal defence guns, situated almost on our track at Merville. After this we soon caught our first sight of the coast; it lay off to port, the promontory north-west of Le Havre. It was with difficulty that we allowed the paratroops to rest with our landfall only fifteen minutes away, but there was no purpose in getting them ready too soon.

We gave the signal for 'action stations' ten minutes before drop-time. Immediately all was bustle and activity, parachutes and kit-bags adjusted and checked, static lines freed and hooked up, each man checking his neighbour's hook and pin. The wireless operator and I took our positions at the back of the fuselage, just to the rear of the open door, ready for the dispatch and to help should there be a stumble, which might easily happen with these men so hung around with cumbersome equipment. The pilot was steadily throttling back to lose height down to 500 feet. The coastline became clear-cut, little white crests of waves breaking on the beach, and there quite suddenly was our villa with its distinctive verandah, just as in the photographs and the model, dead on track! As we passed over the coastline we let go our anti-personnel bombs, to keep the German's heads down, and to make them think we were bombers.

And then to me as I stood at the open door the excitement of picking up the landmarks. The *estaminet* on the coastal road, the farm house with a Dutch barn, that line of poplar trees . . . I knew what crop each field had on it and wondered if they had cut or carried any more of the hay since the last photo had been taken. For a few desperate moments visibility was down to nil as we passed through dust, smoke and haze rising from the bombing of the coastal battery. Then the model and the film came clearly into view again. A certain amount of red tracer flew up in bursts around and about, and what seemed to be white flares appeared on the ground and went out.

The landing lights of the pathfinders were showing plainly ahead of us as the red 4-second warning light came on by the exit door. Paratroopers say this is the longest four seconds in a man's life. The engines are throttled further back, the nose of the aircraft rises slightly, the slope of the floor is towards the rear now. The leader of the stick is silhouetted in the door, arms outstretched at shoulder height, gripping the sides, one foot forward ready to spring; the remainder are crowding and closing up behind him like a queue of strap-hangers waiting to get out of a tube-train in the rush hour. The red light changes to green. Instantly but only as an aid and as reassuring confirmation the dispatcher's hand slaps down hard on Number One's shoulder, he disappears, is gone, another silhouette immediately fills the gap, and is gone . . . like flicking black shadows they go, pouring out almost touching one another, like a pack of cards falling. What a sight! What a moment! Those sixteen paratroopers were out in eight seconds. Two more sticks of sixteen were going down from our numbers 2 and 3, and from the stream of aircraft behind, forty-eight troops every fifteen seconds would be backing them up. The gallant 6th Airborne were pouring, teeming down the sky into action, in the van of the most remarkable of all invasions.

For a moment the great aircraft felt very lonely and empty. The urge to follow those splendid troops was almost irresistible . . . [4]

Follow them he did – nine days later.

Louis Strange Returns to Europe

Early in the battle for the beach-head the 6th Airborne Division had fulfilled its tasks of silencing the Merville Battery, taking bridges over the River Orne and the Caen Canal to ease the Allied advance from the beaches, and destroying others over the Dives to hamper German counter-attack. Since then it had fought a fine holding and harassing action against the strong German forces trying to pierce the Allies' left flank. The American airborne divisions, despite being widely scattered by their transport crews on the night of the invasion, had achieved similar success on the right. But the main force fighting its way inland had not reached its planned objectives. In particular the key town of Caen and its important aerodrome at Carpiquet were still in German hands. Montgomery had thought to take Caen in the first twenty-four hours of the battle. A German Panzer division had thought otherwise.

By 12th June the five 'beaches' had been linked to form a fiercely contested perimeter only some 6 miles from the coast. Within this bridge-head there was an urgent need for airstrips for resupply, the evacuation of wounded and to allow the fighters and fighter-bombers of the 2nd Tactical Air Force to refuel and rearm without having to return to England. Airfield Construction Companies were amongst the earliest support groups to be put ashore, and as soon as they had bulldozed and scraped a bare-earth strip at Bény-sur-Mer, No. 46 Group's 233 Squadron led by Wing Commander Morrison took in the first full lift on 15th June. Louis Strange flew with him, to set up and command the No. 46 Group Advanced Headquarters.

The fleet of twenty Dakotas landed in full view of the enemy, and the thick pall of yellow dust that they raised from the strip pin-pointed their position on the ground. As shells began to fall, the ground equipment and personnel of two Fighter Squadrons were rapidly unloaded, stretchers fixed and 300 wounded taken on board the Dakotas. Two of the aircraft were hit. Within an hour the others were taking off amidst continuing shellfire, then wheeling low out to sea towards England.

Bény-sur-Mer and other rapidly hewn airstrips were quickly occupied by Fighter Squadrons. Others became supply strips, known as Temporary Staging Posts (TSP), each with its own control and handling staff, and a hospital holding unit. Into them poured personnel and the most urgent freight. Out of them were flown the wounded – over 50,000 of them by 46 Group alone during the next three months. The control and local administration of the TSPs was Louis Strange's task.

He set up his Headquarters in the rectory of the village of Magny, 3 miles from Bayeux – and 3 miles from the battlefront . . .

> At night, until one got used to it, the noise of bombing and the crack and bark of our own AA guns was deafening. Streams of incendiary bullets from a low night raider would come down on our landing-strip; the strikes on the ground and houses, the empty shell cases clattering down, sounded like a short sharp hail-storm, over almost as soon as it had begun. We were fairly safe, as everyone who was not under a good stone roof was sleeping deep in a dug-out, which was the first requirement on arrival at a new site in those early beach-head days. [1]

It was at Magny, in the turmoil of battle, that he met the farmer Monsieur L'Étrange and discovered his Norman roots. Wherever his wars took Louis Strange his love of the soil was constantly with him, and his recollections are rarely without a mention of the farming folk and customs of the countryside. In Normandy he was saddened by the widespread destruction of livestock, farm buildings and crops; impressed by the stoicism of those who tended the land.

> I have seen a reaper cutting a lovely field of wheat, just ripe for harvest. Crusader tanks came charging through it, rolling more than half of it flat. The farmer merely halted until they were gone, and then continued to cut what was left. [1]

He soon had six airstrips under his control within the beach-head. Travelling between them on roads congested with military vehicles was a frustration to Louis Strange. He decided to get a horse. In a nearby cherry orchard he found a chestnut mare with an Arab look about her. From the local mayor he heard that she had been left by the Germans, who had taken her in the Ukraine three years before, and who had warned the mayor that he would be shot if the animal wasn't there when they returned from throwing the British back into the sea. Louis assured the mayor the Germans wouldn't be throwing anyone into the sea, gave him a receipt nonetheless, christened the horse 'Cherry' and rode her 6 miles to his billet, bareback, with an old piece of rope for a halter. He said:

> I found her most useful for getting about quickly from one airstrip to another. She would get across country at a nice hand-gallop, and never

seemed to tire. We had to hobble her to a stake in the orchard after a time, because she would keep coming into the Mess tent and taking bread off the table. [1]

The pace of resupply and build-up quickened. Sometimes as many as fifty Dakotas at a time would stream into one of the TSPs, turning onto the loop of peri-track until they filled it nose to tail. Army lorries would back to the opened doors, load, then drive off to be replaced immediately by the waiting ambulances, everyone working flat out with an anxious eye on the sky lest a German aircraft sneak beneath the top cover provided by Allied fighters. Within an hour Pratt and Whitney engines would cough into life again and the first of the Dakotas would turn onto the strip. In clouds of yellow dust one by one they would lift into the sky.

Occasionally Louis would ride to General Richard Gale's Headquarters, set in a stone quarry towards the eastern end of the beach-head, where 6th Airborne Division was still fighting on the left flank. Louis Strange thought it a waste to keep specialist troops in the line, and suggested that they should be withdrawn to prepare for the further airborne 'leaps ahead' that were likely to be required, but Richard Gale insisted that what his men had won they meant to hold. Hold it they did, whilst behind them the Allied force gathered its strength for the break-out from the beach-head.

The heaps of smoking rubble that had once been Caen were finally taken by Canadian troops on 18th July. By then the Americans, to the west, had fought their way across the Cotentin peninsula, had taken Cherbourg against stubborn resistance, and were now pouring through the Avranches 'gap' from the confines of Normandy into more open country beyond, rolling the Germans before them.

In early August, Air Marshal Coningham moved his 2nd Tactical Air Force (TAF) Headquarters from England into the expanding beach-head, positioning it alongside Montgomery's Headquarters at Le Tronquay. Louis Strange moved his own small unit into the same conclave, to represent 46 Group and to play a leading role in the overall co-ordination of increasing air movement. When possible, he and Coningham would dine together and take a little time out of this war to reminisce about the last. The basic principles of interdiction and close support that Coningham had learnt as a Squadron Commander under Louis Strange in 1918 were now being applied by him on a vast scale and with devastating effect. In 1941 his fighter-bombers had been largely responsible for halting Rommel's advance on Cairo and for Montgomery's subsequent victories in the Desert War. Now, in Europe, Air Marshal Sir Arthur Coningham was confirming his reputation as the Second World War's outstanding exponent of tactical air warfare. In addition to harrying the Germans in retreat to the north and west, his rocket-firing Typhoons in particular were now creating havoc amongst some 70,000 of the enemy trapped in the 'Falaise pocket' between the converging American and British Armies.

As the Allied ground forces advanced into mainland Europe, so must their supporting airstrips. Louis Strange moved one of his TSPs up to Évreux, another to Bernay, then prepared to move forward himself. The race for Paris was on. He had been amongst the last RAF officers to leave the French capital in 1940, and he rather wanted to be one of the first to return.

When news came that Allied troops were entering Paris he despatched an advance ground-party under his second-in-command, Squadron Leader the Marquis d'Amodio, who had a house in the Rue Henri Martin that he hoped was still standing, and on 29th August Louis set off after them in an Anson:

> With our personal kit, well armed, and with fuel and rations sufficient for at least a week or two, we left Balleroy with our Anson well up to her full load. It was important to get a staging-post established in Paris at the earliest possible moment, and this was the object of our present flight.
>
> We passed over smashed and battered Caen, and over many villages so bombed and shelled as to be little more than grey scars on the landscape. The area around Falaise was a mass of burnt-out tanks, guns, lorries and equipment. Every road was jammed with traffic going east. Bridges and viaducts had all been bombed or mined, but there was a Bailey Bridge already replacing most of them. Lisieux had been badly hit, but the great white cathedral with its shining dome as large as St Paul's was a fine landmark for all aircrews, and quite untouched. How wonderful it was to be flying once more over this countryside free of enemy aircraft. The last time, when I was flying back the other way, we had sneaked along close to the ground expecting to be bounced at any moment. Now we could with impunity fly right up to the firing-line without any worry at all. 2nd TAF had complete mastery of the air.
>
> It was a great thrill to catch once more the first glimpse of the Eiffel Tower and Paris. It seemed as if the years between had only been a bad dream, except that all the bridges over the Seine, save those in the centre of the city, had long since been destroyed by Bomber Command. We flew past Villacoublay, but as yet there was no airstrip panel out, and the airfield looked just a mass of craters and wrecked hangars. At Orly, however, we found a strip marked out, with enough craters filled in to make a runway, so in we went and landed. Squadron Leader d'Amodio

with a party of No. 18 TSP had already set up a tent and were ready to handle any transport aircraft that might arrive. D'Amodio had already been in to Paris, and had found that his house was quite all right; to his surprise and delight it had not even been looted.

As Orly had been allocated to the Americans, we went at once to General Koenig's Headquarters and made application for Le Bourget to be allocated to British forces. He agreed, but we were told that it was still in enemy hands. There were in fact a great many German troops still in Paris, and a lot of cleaning up was in progress up and down the back streets. The main thoroughfares were, however, quite clear, and filled with excited crowds. The people seemed to be a bit bewildered, as indeed they had good cause to be, and there was not any wild enthusiasm in the greeting they gave the British and American troops just at first. D'Amodio said they were too intent on getting rid of the remaining Germans and rounding up the collaborators.

We tried to get out to Le Bourget later in the afternoon, but the sniping and the gunfire got a bit too warm for our liking, so we turned back and made for the Rue Henri Martin and the Marquis d'Amodio's palatial house. By the time we had got ourselves a good meal from our ration boxes we were too tired to go out again and have a look at liberated Paris night life. The other very good reason for not doing so was that there were far too many stray bullets flying about. In spite of the racket going on all around us, we slept well that night in sumptuously comfortable beds. The thrill of being among the first to return to Paris on the heels of the retreating Germans made the depression we had felt when amongst the last to leave it four years before seem almost worth while.

Early next morning we made our way out to Le Bourget again, and this time we found it clear of the enemy, but what a state it was in! What had not been destroyed by Allied bombing had been finished off by German mines. The airfield and the concrete apron were a mass of craters, and the lovely airport buildings that I and thousands of peacetime travellers had known so well were in an indescribable state. Nevertheless we meant to open it to air traffic again somehow. The RAF Ensign was run up over the control tower on 30th August at 10 o'clock in the morning. [1]

It would be several days before an Airfield Construction Company could be expected to reach Le Bourget. Louis Strange wasn't prepared to wait that long to have the airfield ready to receive the first transports. Quite unofficially he persuaded the local Maquis to bring in gangs of German prisoners and French collaborators to remove the debris, fill in the craters, and make the least damaged buildings habitable. Within twenty-four hours the TSP at Le Bourget was in operation.

Louis then flew back to Normandy to report to 2nd TAF and by telephone link to Transport Command and his own 46 Group Headquarters. He placed urgent requests for men and materials to create further staging-posts, for the advance into Europe was now moving at such pace that the spearhead formations were in danger of outrunning their supply system. The Germans had been expected to make a stand on the Seine, or further back on the Somme, but had been harried across both rivers with no chance to hold and regroup. As Montgomery's 21st Army Group raced northwards on a track parallel to the Channel coast, to his right the US 1st Army under Lieutenant General Hodges was also across the Seine and probing the Ardennes, while further south Patton's US 3rd Army was approaching Metz and the gateway to Lorraine. A further US Army Group was moving up the Rhône Valley from its landings in southern France. The armoured columns spearheading these advances needed fuel, ammunition and air cover. That in turn required forward airstrips, for with the bulk of supplies still coming through the improvised harbours along the Normandy beaches, the road links were over-stretched.

Louis Strange moved his advanced Headquarters out of Paris and into Amiens, where on a grass strip a constant stream of Dakotas was bringing in fuel in jerrycans to keep the tanks of 30th Armoured Corps moving and the fighters of 2nd TAF flying. At Amiens he was told that with an expanding range of command, his unit was now advanced to Wing status – No. 111 Wing. In that case, Louis demanded, could he have some more staff officers to run the damn thing?

Arras, Reims, Lille, Mons fell to the Allies. The Belgian border was crossed. Brussels was now the target. And amongst the first airmen into the capital? Of course . . .

As soon as he heard that British tanks were in the outskirts of Brussels, Louis Strange once more despatched Squadron Leader d'Amodio with an advance ground party, and at 1600 hours on 4th September followed them from Amiens in his Anson. It was a route he had first flown in 1914 in his Henry Farman, when the first four Squadrons of the RFC had moved up from Amiens to the old airfield at Maubeuge. It took him over the old trench lines and the orderly ranks of white tombstones in the military cemeteries of his first war; past Vimy Ridge off his left wing and Le Câteau on his right; above the killing grounds of Cambrai where young Ben and his SE-5 had been swallowed by the churned soil.

From Mons to Brussels he kept close to the main road, mindful of the German stragglers who still posed a threat in open countryside. Allied lorries and tanks thronged the route, moving through villages thick with flags and cheering crowds. Then over the Lion of Waterloo flew the Anson with the sun setting behind it and Brussels ahead, smoke rising from the dome of the Palais de Justice, and the twinkle of shell bursts out to the east of the city against a darkening horizon. It was in that direction they flew – to the city's airport at Évère, well known to Louis as the home of Belgium's civil airline SABENA before the war. With undercarriage down, he searched for an airstrip identification panel, but was met instead by an uncomfortably accurate burst of anti-aircraft fire. Down among the chimneys and back across the city they went: they had arrived too early. Louis made for the airfield at Nivelles to the south of Brussels, but finding it obstructed by poles and fencing, landed in a nearby stubble-field.

Uncertain whether he would be greeted by Belgian kisses or German bullets, Louis Strange kept the engines running until a boy on a bicycle appeared to tell him that although there was still fighting going on and there were still Germans in the woods, Nivelles was in the hands of the Belgian Resistance. Apparently the British armoured columns had by-passed the small town, which had proceeded to liberate itself. Louis was taken into Nivelles in a cart, covered to hide his Air Force blue uniform lest someone mistake it for German grey in the fading light. They passed at one point through fierce gunfire, but eventually linked up with the local Resistance leader who gave Louis a guard for the Anson, accommodation for the night and the promise of armed escort into Brussels on the following morning.

Before going into the city, Louis indulged in a small selfishness. He had a visit to make. In 1918, on the heels of the defeated Germans, he had personally 'liberated' the nearby Château Lillois, home of the Comte de Meuss, and had later established his 51 Wing Headquarters there. He now directed the small convoy of captured staff-cars, bristling with machine-guns and Belgian flags, to the gates of the château, then went to the house on foot and rang the bell. It was opened by a girl who swept the Englishman back twenty-four years, for she was the image of the Comtesse who had opened the door to him on that previous occasion. He recovered from his surprise to realise that it must be her elder daughter. 'Hello Jacqueline,' he said. 'Is your mother at home? Tell her Colonel Strange has called.'

He could not linger with the astonished yet rapturous family that he had 'liberated' in both world wars. Escorted by his Resistance fighters, he hastened to join the route of the main British advance into Brussels. The fight for the city was over, the road now lined with riotous welcome:

158

There was hardly room for the vehicles to get along the narrow path between the surging crowds on both sides. Lorries and tanks could hardly be seen for the masses of civilians riding on them waving and cheering, and hugging and kissing the troops. What a scene – one that could never be forgotten by those who took part in it. All through the city it was like the densest football crowd ever seen, swaying, singing and cheering continously. The applause and cheering reminded me of nothing so much as the roar at Twickenham with the English forwards charging down the field on to the Scottish line in the Calcutta Cup . . . [1]

His Resistance men took him to the Astoria Hotel where, as pre-arranged, he met Squadron Leader d'Amodio with a rather shot-up RAF staff-car. Louis thanked his Belgian escort, hung a sign '111 Wing RAF' on the hotel door, and drove with D'Amodio to Évère, now cleared of Germans. With white fabric strips they were able to mark a reasonable runway between the craters, then went back to Nivelles, flew the Anson out of its stubble-field, and landed at Évère. Then it was back to Brussels, to find 30 Corps headquarters in the grounds of the Domaine Royale and signal 2nd TAF that Évère was open for the first transports to fly in.

As he fell asleep in the Astoria Hotel at the end of that memorable day, Louis Strange wondered if he would be staying longer in Brussels than he had in Paris . . .

Although advanced units pushed on towards the Dutch border, the momentum of the Allied advance was beginning to slow. With the Channel ports either still held by pockets of stubborn German resistance or with their docks damaged beyond immediate repair, the bulk of supplies and reinforcement for 47 Allied Divisions (2 million men) was still coming into the original beach-head, now over 300 miles from the forward units. Road supply of the British Armies also suffered from the withdrawal of 1,400 lorries to which wrong gearbox components had been fitted. The delivery of urgent supplies, particularly of fuel, fell increasingly upon the air transport system. It wasn't enough to keep the Allied Armies moving forward at the pace that had taken them from the beach-head to the Dutch border in five weeks. And as the Allied advance slackened, German resistance quickened.

Anticipating that his stay in Brussels might after all be prolonged and that the Astoria Hotel would soon be claimed by more imposing units than his, Louis Strange sought alternative accommodation for No. 111 Wing:

With this in mind we drove out to Boisfort, and I stopped at the house of another old friend of 1918, Monsieur Benoît, the burgomaster at that

159

time, close to the racecourse, hoping that I would find him alive and well, although I knew he would now be well over eighty. My hopes were realised; he came himself to the door and we recognised each other at once. As on my appearance at the Château Lillois I was kissed soundly on both cheeks, again and again, with even more fervour, though less softly. '*Ha, mon brave, mon colonel – le colonel Strange lui-même!*' He capered round in great delight, as lively as a kitten. The war had not got Georges Benoît down. The champagne corks were soon popping. *Vive les Anglais! Vive Belgique* [sic]! *Vive* everyone . . . [1]

Monsieur Benoît ensured that 'colonel' Strange and his Headquarters received the best accommodation and comforts that Boisfort could provide.

In mid-September Louis Strange flew to London for a meeting with his new AOC, Air Commodore Darvall, and to spend a night with Marjorie in their Kensington flat, from which Marjorie was car-driving for the Women's Voluntary Service and where she was far less frightened than Louis of the German V2 rockets now targeted on the city.

He flew back to Normandy, thence in an Auster to Brussels, calling at Paris and his other TSPs on the way. In Brussels he found that he was now a Group Captain – a promotion that caused him a wry smile, for his RAFVR substantive rank remained that of Squadron Leader and his previous experience of acting rank was that it didn't last long. What pleased him more was that his demands for support had been answered and he now had two Wing Commanders on his staff, including his old friend Tony Dudgeon. He also had a Squadron of Dakotas based at Évère – No. 271 – not actually under his command, but as far as he was concerned, as good as. That he still operated beyond his authority and not always with the approval of his masters was noted by his colleague from Ringway and Netheravon days, Lawrence Wright, who whilst serving back at Group Headquarters wrote, 'A slightly tired look, I noticed, came over the face of Air Commodore Darvall when Louis' name was mentioned.' [2]

That tired look may have originated with Louis Strange's reaction to the plans for Operation 'Market Garden', on which the AOC had briefed him during that short visit to 46 Group Headquarters. Rather than advance on a broad front against the Germans, now consolidated along the line of the Albert Canal, Montgomery decided on a powerful thrust by his 2nd British Army deep into Holland, then a right swing into the heart of Germany itself. The carpet along which this thrust would roll would be laid by airborne forces. American Airborne Divisions would secure the crossings of the waterways beyond

Eindhoven and at Nijmegen, and the British 1st Airborne Division would take and hold the key bridge across the Lower Rhine – at Arnhem. Firstly Louis objected to the withdrawal of almost the entire transport fleet for this operation, not only because of the severe disruption to supply, but because the cessation of transport flights would surely signal to the Germans that a massive airborne operation was pending. He also expressed strong reservations about the plan for the assault on Arnhem. Since the pioneering of British airborne forces at Ringway he had supported the view that successful assault from the sky depended upon surprise and swiftness of execution: these in turn depended upon rapid concentration of force on drop zones as close as possible to, if not actually on, the target. He was appalled to learn that at Arnhem the 1st Airborne Division was to be dropped in daylight, over a period of three days, 7 miles from the bridge, and with what he saw as an inadequate plan for close air support. His concern made no dent in the over-optimism that launched such a venture. Little opposition was expected, he was told, and in any case the airborne boys would have to hold the bridge for only two days, which was as long as it would take for the 2nd Army to reach the Rhine.

He – and others who viewed the planning as dangerously inadequate – could do nothing but support the operation to the best of their ability. By glider and parachute the troops went in on 17th September. The American 101st Airborne Division quickly secured the crossings of the waterways at the southern end of the carpet. Further north at Nijmegen, their colleagues of the 82nd Airborne had to fight more fiercely to take the bridge over the Waal. Louis Strange's role was the resupply of the 82nd. He sent Tony Dudgeon off with a jeep, a revolver and a radio beacon with which to guide the Dakotas into the drop zone, and as soon as possible, he flew into the battle area himself in an Auster. Then, from a frustrating distance, he watched his fears for 1st Airborne Division realised. Poor communications and an intelligence scenario that had failed to recognise the presence in Arnhem of heavily armed Panzer units compounded the problems that Louis Strange and others had foreseen. Only the 750 men of John Frost's 2nd Battalion reached the bridge before the rest of the Division was trapped at Oosterbeek with its back to the Rhine. Even so, John Frost and his paratroopers held the northern end of the bridge for the two days it should have taken the tanks of the 2nd Army to reach them, and then for almost two days more before being overwhelmed by vastly superior numbers and firepower. When the 2nd Army reached the Rhine – five days after its target date – of the 10,000 men who had landed at Arnhem, 7,000 were dead or captured. Louis Strange wept for them.

Tony Dudgeon said of Louis Strange at that time that his ideas for the use of transport aircraft for support of ground forces were as farsighted as had been his concept of tactical strike in the First World War. 'He was, as ever, ahead of his time . . .'[3]

As the depleted Dakota force recovered from its own losses during 'Market Garden' and as the Allies pushed into Holland more slowly than had been hoped, the aerial convoys began to pour into the forward areas again. At the height of the resupply into Évère, Louis Strange watched 435 Dakotas land, offload and take off again in the space of six hours. There were busy times on the ground too, laying and pegging PSP (pierced steel plating) over the airstrips before summer dust turned to autumn mud. Although it wasn't a standard procedure, Louis Strange had the PSP laid on straw wherever he could. He chose to build his own strips rather than share airfields with the forward Fighter Squadrons, for he rarely saw eye-to-eye with their commander, Air Marshal Harry Broadhurst, who considered that transport aircraft had no place in forward areas, and who threatened to have Tony Dudgeon arrested when he found him almost in the combat zone preparing to receive resupply.

Some of the pressure was taken off No. 111 Wing by the creation of a sister formation – No. 110 Wing – based in Paris, to relieve Louis Strange of the TSPs in the rear areas.

Busy though he and his units were, as ever Louis Strange found time for fun. He was proud of his Mess at Boisfort, and of his Guest Nights which were well provided with captured German wines. They were usually held on a Sunday evening after the races which the Belgians had quickly re-established on the Boisfort course, with fine horses that had been abandoned by the Germans. To these evenings Louis invited many of those he had entertained in similar circumstances in 1918: Monsieur Benoît, the burgomaster; General Oosterchrist; Monsieur and Madame Lelon, who had been much involved in the escape lines for Allied aircrew; Prosper Cocquet, who Louis had known as chief pilot for SABENA before the war, and the Comte and Comtesse de Meuss, of course.

Cherry, like a good camp-follower, had come up with the baggage trucks from Normandy. One day in October Louis Strange rode her across country to Château Lillois to attend the wedding of the Comte's second daughter Guenevière. And there he left Cherry, as a wedding gift.

It may be that someone in authority had recalled Louis Strange's outspoken criticisms of the planning for Arnhem, and with hindsight had recognised their validity. In early November, a signal was handed to him in his office at Boisfort. It told him that he was posted, immediately, to Headquarters 1st Allied Airborne Army. He was to be part of the staff that would plan any future airborne operations in Europe.

The 1st Allied Airborne Army, now comprising four American and the two British Airborne Divisions, was commanded by the American Lieutenant General Lewis Brereton who, as a staff officer in 1918 had transposed General Billy Mitchell's visionary concept for an airborne assault on Metz into a feasible but unrealised plan. Louis Strange was appointed to him as Assistant Deputy Chief of Staff, Plans, RAF. The US Army, US Army Air Force and the British Army were similarly represented.

The wry smile that Louis had assumed a month earlier when promoted to acting rank of Group Captain appeared to be justified, for his posting to Allied Airborne Army required him to revert to Wing Commander. Lewis Brereton couldn't understand it. In the US Army, a man of Louis Strange's experience and ability would have been a General, he told Headquarters Transport Command. Air-Chief Marshal Sir Frederick Bowhill wrote to him personally to explain the intricacies of acting and substantive rank and the limitations on promotion within the RAFVR. Lewis Brereton replied that he still didn't understand it; Strange should be a full Colonel at least. Transport Command sighed and gave Louis Strange back his acting rank of Group Captain. Louis no doubt smiled another wry smile and got on with the war.

The Headquarters occupied a mansion in park-like surroundings close to Ascot racecourse. The staff was predominantly American. Once he got used to the blaring of radios and the clatter of fruit-machines in the Mess, and when he had learnt their language, Louis Strange enjoyed and admired the Americans. He liked their confidence and their energy and their rations. He got on particularly well with his younger USAAF counterpart, former fighter pilot Colonel Phil Cochran, who had won a reputation for unconventional and dashing leadership in his command of the mixed bag of fighters, light bombers, transports and gliders that had so effectively supported the long-range penetrations into Japanese-held Burma by Orde Wingate's jungle fighters, the famed 'Chindits'. He too was new to the staff, and it was said that had he and Louis Strange been there for the planning of 'Market Garden', the outcome might have been different. With Lieutenant Colonel Baird representing the British Army and Colonel Birburn the US Army, they were a good team.

Just as they were settling at Ascot, Lewis Brereton decided to establish an advanced Headquarters in Paris, under his deputy,

General Cutler. The planning team and Louis Strange went with it. Offices were established in the Hôtel Royale at Maisons-Laffitte, outside the city and close to Eisenhower's Supreme Headquarters Allied Expeditionary Force (SHAEF), conveniently close also to yet another racecourse and its well-stocked stables, from which Louis was soon taking a dawn ride each morning. He also had a little L-5 communications aircraft at his disposal, in which to fly between the various Headquarters and units associated with the planning of airborne operations. Life at Maisons-Laffitte was pleasant. But busy.

The task of the planning team was to prepare not just for actual airborne assaults, but to plan in advance for potential operations; for any situation in which airborne forces might be used to ease and support the advance of the land forces now pressing in on Germany. The likely routes of that advance were examined in detail, likely obstacles and lines of defence recognised, likely battle scenarios envisaged. If airborne assault might profitably play a part in those scenarios, the size of force required, the method of delivery and drop zone locations were planned in detail. The capture of airfields, the securing of river crossings, the blocking of potential lines of German retreat featured high amongst the plans for the use of the waiting Airborne Divisions. The plans would then be put on the shelf to be revised, implemented or discarded as required.

One possibility not planned for by SHAEF was Hitler's final gamble for victory. In late December, Von Runstedt's 5th and 6th Panzer Armies, under cover of poor weather, struck through the Ardennes in a bold attempt to reach the Channel ports and split the Allied Armies in two. It almost succeeded. A 50-mile gap was torn in the thinly held American lines. Into that gap were rushed the American 101st and 82nd Divisions and smaller British elements of the 1st Allied Airborne Army. In epic fighting they held Bastogne and St-Vith, and as the 1st and 3rd US Armies began to squeeze the flanks of the threatening 'bulge', Hitler was eventually forced to order Von Runstedt to withdraw his Panzers before they were crushed. The Allies breathed again.

In mid-January the great Russian offensive on Germany's eastern front poured over the Vistula, whilst in the west the British and American Armies, now receiving bulk supply through the recaptured port of Antwerp, began to roll forward again. And at last Allied Airborne Army Headquarters was able to take one of its plans off the shelf. The top-secret file was labelled Operation 'Varsity'. It was the plan to deploy the British 6th and the American 17th Airborne Divisions to secure the woods and the high ground east of the Rhine at

Wesel in support of a large-scale amphibious crossing of the river by Montgomery's 21st Army.

The lessons of Arnhem had been learnt. At dawn on 24th March, some 21,700 airborne troops landed by parachute and glider on top of their targets in one massive delivery by 1,696 transport aircraft. With well directed close air support, the troops achieved their objectives and linked up with main ground forces within twenty-four hours, as planned. As Louis Strange closed the file on 'Varsity' and its 21,700 men, he reflected on the five old Whitleys and the forty-four troops tumbling from their bellies in front of Winston Churchill in 1941. They had come a long way in four years . . .

The crossing of the Rhine was the last of the great airborne assaults. But that wasn't known at the time. The war wasn't over. Further strikes from the sky might hasten its end. There were other files to be updated by the planning team, new ones to be begun. There was Operation 'Arena', a bold project that bore all the marks of Cochran and Strange in its intention to deliver all six Airborne Divisions to create an 'air-head' midway between the Ruhr and Berlin, into which other Infantry Divisions could be flown. Operation 'Eclipse' proposed an airborne assault on Berlin itself. They and

Louis Strange was the RAF representative on General Brereton's planning staff for the massive airborne assault in support of the crossing of the Rhine in the closing stages of the war (*Photo: No. 1 Parachute Training School*)

165

others were not launched, mainly because the Allied advance into Germany was regaining a momentum that neither required nor allowed time for airborne assistance.

As Hitler's defences crumbled on both Eastern and Western fronts, the planning staff at Maisons-Laffitte looked to the provision of relief and possible protection for prisoners of war (POWs) left by the retreating Germans. Plans were made to drop medical and other supplies to the prison camps, to deliver Special Air Service teams and parachute battalions if needed, and to fly prisoners out where possible. Louis Strange was attached to SHAEF Headquarters at Reims to co-ordinate these mini-operations. Many of the supply drops went ahead, but fortunately only the eighteen parachutists of a Special Forces unit, Operation 'Violet', were required for POW protection. From hastily prepared airstrips close to the camps, however, Dakotas flew several thousand liberated prisoners to freedom. To Louis Strange who planned them and to the aircrews who flew them, these mercy missions brought a particular glow of satisfaction as the war drew to its close. Louis was also on the spot for the final act of the drama.

On 4th May 1945, on Lüneburg Heath, Montgomery took the surrender of Germany's North-Western Armies. On the evening of the 6th, with the Russians in Berlin and the Americans linked with them on the Elbe, a string of staff-cars drove into the courtyard of the former Agricultural College in Reims that housed SHAEF Forward Headquarters. Leaving desks and telephones and files, out onto the verandah that ran round the square poured the staff of the Headquarters, Louis Strange amongst them. He watched two figures emerge from the second car, one in field grey, the other in naval uniform. General Alfred Jodl and Admiral Friedeburg had come to negotiate final surrender on all fronts. The staff lingered on the verandah until the early hours of 7th May when Jodl and Friedeburg left, and the signal went out from SHAEF, 'The mission of this Allied Force was fulfilled at 0241, local time, May 7, 1945.'

Louis Strange wrote:

> It took a little time for the fact that the war was over and won to sink in, but when it did, it was well and truly celebrated in Reims. Could a better spot in all Europe be found to celebrate victory than the centre of a province of France renowned throughout the world for the excellence of its champagne wine? [1]

CHAPTER FIFTEEN

The End of the Flight

On 9th June 1945 Louis Strange flew from Villacoublay to North Weald, where he was given immediate leave pending demobilisation, which in his case was quickly processed.

He left the Service quietly, tired, pleased that it was all over – pleased in particular that his son Brian had survived the conflict in Europe and the Far East, and that Susan had survived what her father saw as even greater hazards from hitch-hiking about the country throughout the war years and a marriage to which he would not have given his approval had she sought it. Susan was a spirited rebel, just like her father.

Earlier in the year Louis Strange had been awarded the OBE. Not enough, thought many. Lewis Brereton, in particular, considered him to have been poorly rewarded by his own country for his creative achievements throughout the war and particularly for his contribution to Airborne Forces. He gave his own recognition to Louis Strange by personally writing the citation that brought him the American Bronze Star Medal:

> Through his tireless energy, devotion to duty, technical and practical knowledge of aircraft, and wide experience in the operational employment of aircraft and airborne troops, Wing Commander Strange rendered a major contribution to the successful accomplishment of airborne operations against the enemy during the period 14 December 1944 until the cessation of hostilities in Europe.

Robert Smith Barry didn't think it was enough, either, and wrote to numerous senior officers to say so. He returned briefly to England in 1945 to marry Anne Garnier, who wrote, 'Louis Strange insisted on coming to our very small wedding – he suddenly got up and talked for twenty minutes on what Bob had done. It was most moving.' [1] It was the last time the two old rebels would meet. Smith Barry set up home in Natal, where he died in 1949 after an operation on the leg that he had shattered in that 1914 crash. That damned BE-8 had got him after all, Louis reminisced.

Louis Strange was fifty-four when he left the Royal Air Force for the second time. Young at heart, not prepared to 'retire' from anything, he applied himself with apparently undiminished vigour to his twin loves: farming and flying. He farmed for a while at Little Fishers Farm near Chichester before taking an extended holiday in South Africa, which he didn't like, then returning to live for a while in Bognor Regis.

His return to civil flying in 1945 was initially through resumption of his co-directorship of the Straight Corporation. He became director of Exeter and Plymouth airports, and was much involved in the re-establishment of Western Airways and Straight Aviation Training. Surplus Ansons were purchased and converted for civilian use as carriers and navigation trainers, and several Fairchild Arguses obtained. In 1946 the small independent airlines were nationalised to form British European Airways, and Louis Strange ceased his association with Western Airways but increased his links with Straight Corporation's airports and aero clubs in the south-west. He was also at this time Managing Director of the Hampshire School of Flying and of the Hants Aero Club. When the club faced extinction, he bought it, inspired by sentiment rather than financial wisdom, and despite strong opposition from Marjorie.

Through these positions in civil aviation and at every opportunity that came his way, he continued to preach the spirit of air adventure. Addressing the first annual dinner of the Dorchester branch of the RAF Association in 1947, he said:

> It is the spirit of air adventure I want you to encourage – in the Air
> Training Corps and in any way you can. If you can see any possibility of
> starting some kind of club, maybe only a glider club if you can find some
> up-currents around Maiden Castle, that is the thing that will help you to
> help the youth of Dorchester get into the air . . . [2]

He practised what he preached – getting into the air whenever he could. He bought a twelve-year-old Auster Taylorcraft for £250 and in 1950 flew it in the *Daily Express* Challenge Trophy Air Race. At the age of fifty-nine he was the oldest of the seventy-six pilots who entered the race along the southern coast of England, and as a 'veteran of the two world wars' he attracted more publicity in the national press than did the race itself. He also took Marjorie for a holidaying tour of Europe in the Taylorcraft, and on occasions took his ninety-year-old aunt Ellen – 'Nellie' – for flips over the countryside of Wiltshire and Dorset they both knew and loved so well.

During the late 1940s Louis Strange had begun to write his *Further Recollections of an Airman*, an account of his service during the Second World War. Although the manuscript contains episodes as dramatic and as well related as those in his 1933 book, it does not have

Aunt Nellie Strange with Louis beside his Auster Taylorcraft

the sustained vigour and spirit of his earlier writing. It contains more passages of personal reflection, and expresses opinions on political and military affairs that were considered too extreme by the publishers to whom he submitted the work. It was politely rejected. A good editing might have taken it into print, but Louis was not a man to compromise. Better written was his account of family history, and of a happy childhood and early farming ventures before flying lured him away from the valley of the Stour. He called it *A Strange Story as I've Heard Tell*. Apparently he never submitted it for publication.

In 1952 Louis Strange lapsed into a prolonged period of ill health. His physical disabilities and the financial losses that he had inherited with the Hants Aero Club plunged him into deep depressions. He sold his aeroplane, resigned his directorships, and withdrew altogether from Straight Corporation – by that time renamed Airways Union. His depression became manic. Without consulting him, Marjorie arranged for Louis to be consigned to West Sussex Hospital. He found himself confined amongst the certified insane of the hospital's D Block. After the obligatory week of virtual imprisonment he was examined and declared decidedly odd, but not mad. He discharged himself, fled to Wincanton, where for £160 he bought a dilapidated cottage, and never went near his wife again. Louis had always been a difficult man to keep pace with, had maintained an eye for the ladies

169

and had become increasingly exasperating with the years. Marjorie made no great attempt to lure him home.

He spent four frugal years at Campson Cottage, living on his pension – poor but contented, his daughter Susan recalls. Material possessions had never attracted him: he was happy to be without responsibility and to be close to the land. Every day he walked or went searching for his inseparable and ever-wandering dogs, a Jack Russell and a Lurcher called Nipper and Buster, watched badgers, stole turnips, and followed local hunts in his car, his sympathies now much with the fox. He went often to Worth Matravers to give his brother and two nephews unwanted advice on how to run the family farm. He always had been far too innovative and outspoken for most of his farming contemporaries, who through him a bit of a crank. Grass-drying, for example . . . He had long deplored the wastage in labour and in grass itself by traditional means of haymaking, and even in the 1930s had foreseen a machine that could 'go into a field at any time of day or night and lift, dry, grind, cube and put into bags, any green crop' [3]. So after the war he produced a prototype grass-drier. He obtained a Whittle jet-engine, and with the aid of aircraft engineer Marcus Langley, converted it into a paraffin-driven grass-drier

Louis Strange at the 1958 Reunion of the Merchant Ships Fighter Unit (from left to right: Douglas Grant, John MacDonald, Michael Lyne, John Pickwell, Louis Strange, Harry Ball-Wilson, Sydney Ward, Arthur Giggins, Basil Tatham, Peter Mallet)

Louis Strange showing his First World War log-book to Officer Commanding No. 23 Squadron, Wing Commander Chapman, at Coltishall in 1959

capable of processing 15 cwt of green grass in an hour. The rate was uneconomical, but could have been improved to a viable output had support for the project been forthcoming. It wasn't. As usual, Louis Strange was ahead of his time.

As his health revived, as it so often did when he walked away from the doctors and back to the land, he resumed his club flying, mostly in hired planes out of Hurn airport and Thruxton. But increasingly his association with the world of aviation was through its social functions and reunions, at which he was often a revered guest. In 1956 he was admitted into the Freedom of the Guild of Air Pilots and Air Navigators, and would continue to take his seat at its prestigious annual banquet into the 1960s. In 1957 he flew to Wunstorf in Germany to attend the disbandment of No. 5 Squadron, with whom he had fought on the Western Front in 1914. On that visit he flew in and took the controls of a jet-fighter for the first time – a dual Vampire. 'A bit different from my old Henry Farman . . .', he said to the young jet jockey alongside him.

There were reunions of the Central Flying School, of the dwindling survivors of the Royal Flying Corps, of the Merchant Ships Fighter Unit Association, of Airborne Forces, and of the Squadrons with which he had flown or that he had administered. In 1959 he was guest of honour at the reunion of No. 23 Squadron, the Squadron that he had formed in 1915. He flew up to RAF Coltishall from Thruxton in a hired plane to be a guest of No. 23 again at the Station's Battle of Britain Day in 1960. His journey prompted him to write to *The Post*:

> Will there never be any spot in Dorset that an aeroplane can land on or take off from without having first obtained special permission or having to report a criminal offence to the police? Have I always to motor 60 miles to hire an air taxi as I did last Saturday to fly myself from the Wiltshire Flying Club's aerodrome near Andover to be present at the Coltishall flying display, Norwich? I did it in two hours, flying a Tiger Moth, far quicker than by road. It only used 13 gallons of petrol to do 200 miles with no possibility of a puncture, no gears to change, no cross roads, and I didn't see a policeman once . . .'

It was one of his last recorded flights. He was sixty-eight years old.

By that time he had moved to Winterbourne Kingston, living in a caravan whilst having a house built to his own design. The design would today be called 'environmentally friendly'. Then, it was considered eccentric. He inevitably fell foul of the local planning authority.

Although the land had revived him, there were further periods of hospitalisation for recurring bouts of manic depression. The electric-shock treatment that he received in Guy's Hospital before he walked out – threatening to do so naked if they didn't return his clothes – and later at Bournemouth, could only have intensified his terror of confinement and of the mental disintegration that sometimes threatened.

Joy Wooton, who had been his landlady during his time at Ringway, had moved to Worth Matravers to be close to Louis. He visited frequently, and eventually moved into her cottage to spend the last years of his life with her. He spent time too with his daughter Susan, now farming near Tring. Her husband Cliff was farming correspondent for the *Observer* and strong in scientific theory, against which Louis – a traditional 'organic farmer' – argued vehemently. At Worth Matravers he still helped and sometimes hindered his nephews Peter and John, who had continued to farm the family land when Ronald had died in 1955. He still wrote letters to the local Press extolling the spirit of air adventure and demanding aerodromes for Dorsetshire. He still smiled wryly when accounts – usually distorted – of his adventures appeared in flying magazines and aviation histories.

His fame became increasingly associated with his tussle with the inverted Martinsyde in 1915 and his escape from Merville in the

Hurricane in 1940, and less with his real achievements as leader and pioneer in so many fields of aviation. Those two particular escapades had been featured in real-life comic-strips in the popular magazine *Top Spot* in 1959. But he wouldn't have minded that. He would rather be remembered for those long-ago adventures, for they spoke of the spirit of the air, and that was far more important than the dry facts of aviation history. Far more important than all the bumf . . .

His daughter Susan knew that her father was coming to the end of his long flight when he stopped arguing with Cliff. He quietened even further after the death of his dogs, Nipper and Buster.

Louis Arbon Strange died quietly in his sleep in 1966, at the age of seventy-five. He was buried in the cemetery of St Nicholas Church at Worth Matravers, close to his parents, and in the midst of the land that they had farmed, and is farmed still by his great-nephews John, David and Ronald Strange. Ronald bears a striking resemblance to photographs of the young Louis, standing seriously by his Blériot or the Grahame-White biplane at Hendon.

On Louis Strange's now weathered tombstone in that quiet country churchyard are lines from Psalm 139:

> If I take the wings of the morning
> Thy right hand shall hold me . . .

REFERENCES

Chapter One

[1] Louis Strange, *A Strange Story as I've Heard Tell* (unpublished)
[2] Louis Strange, *Recollections of an Airman* (John Hamilton, 1933); republished by Greenhill Books (Vintage Aviation Library, 1989)

Chapter Two

[1] Louis Strange, *Recollections of an Airman*
[2] *Daily Mail*, 22nd June 1914

Chapter Three

[1] Louis Strange, *Recollections of an Airman*
[2] Group Captain Carmichael, 'No. 5 Squadron', *Flight* (18th October 1957)
[3] Cecil Lewis, *Sagittarius Rising* (Peter David, 1936)
[4] Louis Strange's first log-book, May 1914–August 1919
[5] Louis Strange, *Farming and Flying* (unpublished)

Chapter Four

[1] Louis Strange, *Recollections of an Airman*
[2] Group Captain Carmichael, 'No. 5 Squadron'
[3] Louis Strange's first log-book
[4] Ira Jones, *An Air Fighter's Scrap Book* (Nicholson and Watson, 1938)
[5] Shane Leslie, *Memoirs of Gordon Shepherd* (Hazell, Watson and Viney, 1924)

Chapter Five

[1] Harry Ward to author, 1988
[2] Louis Strange, *Recollections of an Airman*
[3] Letter from Robert Smith Barry to W A Ramsay, 1945

Chapter Six

[1] James T B McCudden, *Flying Fury* (Greenhill Books, 1973)
[2] A H Cobby, *High Adventure* (Kookaburra Technical Publications, 1965)
[3] Louis Strange, *Recollections of an Airman*
[4] Louis Strange's first log-book

Chapter Seven

[1] Louis Strange, *Recollections of an Airman*
[2] Louis Strange's first log-book
[3] Louis Strange, *A Stange Story as I've Heard Tell*
[4] Louis Strange, 'London to Berlin Non-Stop', *Flight* (10th January 1929)
[5] *Flight* (3rd January 1929)
[6] Louis Strange, *Farming and Flying*
[7] Cyril Tubbs to author, 1990

Chapter Eight

[1] Straight Aviation Training Ltd brochure, 1936
[2] Louis Strange, *Farming and Flying*
[3] Louis Strange, *Recollections of an Airman*
[4] Louis Strange, 'Flying Progress 1910–1937', *Straightaway* (July 1937)

Chapter Nine

[1] Louis Strange, *Further Recollections of an Airman* (unpublished)
[2] Letter from Whitney Straight to Louis Strange, 6th June 1940
[3] Letter from Harold Balfour to Louis Strange, 29th May 1940
[4] Letter from Bill Courtenay to Louis Strange, 22nd June 1940
[5] Letter from H E Lowrey to Louis Strange, 20th June 1940

Chapter Ten

[1] Louis Strange, *Further Recollections of an Airman*
[2] Lawrence Wright, *The Wooden Sword* (Elek, London, 1967)
[3] Robert Fender to author, 1988
[4] Harry Ward, *The Yorkshire Birdman* (Robert Hale Ltd, 1990)

Chapter Eleven

[1] Louis Strange, *Further Recollections of an Airman*
[2] Ralph Barker, *The Hurricats* (Pelham, 1978)
[3] Alec Lumsden to author, 1992
[4] Air Marshal Michael Lyne to author, 1991

Chapter Twelve

[1] Louis Strange, *Further Recollections of an Airman*
[2] Letters from Robert Smith Barry to W A Ramsay, 1945–6
[3] Richard Townshend Bickers to author, 1991, and in *The First Great Air War* (Hodder and Stoughton, 1988)

Chapter Thirteen

[1] Air Vice-Marshal Dudgeon to author, 1992
[2] HQ 46 Group letter, 27th July 1944
[3] Lawrence Wright, *The Wooden Sword*
[4] Louis Strange, *Further Recollections of an Airman*

Chapter Fourteen

[1] Louis Strange, *Further Recollections of an Airman*
[2] Lawrence Wright, *The Wooden Sword*
[3] Air Vice-Marshal Tony Dudgeon to author, 1992

Chapter Fifteen

[1] F D Tredrey, *Pioneer Pilot* (Peter Davies, 1976)
[2] Louis Strange, address to the Dorchester RAF Association, January 1947
[3] Louis Strange, *Farming and Flying*

INDEX

177

178

181

Printed in the United Kingdom for HMSO
Dd 0297407   C30   5/94